THE MONK OF MOUNT ATHOS

THE MONK OF
MOUNT ATHOS

Staretz Silouan 1866–1938

by
ARCHIMANDRITE SOPHRONY

Translated from the Russian
by
Rosemary Edmonds

St. Vladimir's Seminary Press
Crestwood, New York 10707

Excerpted from the Library of Congress Catalog

Sofronii, Archimandrite, 1896-1993
     The Monk of Mount Athos: Staretz Silouan, 1866-1938 / by
Archimandrite Sophrony : translated from the Russian by Rosemary Edmonds.
ISBN 978-0-91383-615-6

BX597.S48 S34 2001
271'.819'092 B   LCCN: 99034265

First Published 1973
by A.R. Mowbray & Co Ltd
The Alden Press, Osney Mead
Oxford, OX2 OEG

This is a revised edition, with additional material of THE UNDISTORTED
IMAGE which was published in 1958 and based on a translation and
adaptation of the original (1948) Russian text, STARETZ SILOUAN,
published Paris 1952

First printing 1975
Second printing 1989
Third printing 2020

THE MONK OF MOUNT ATHOS

ST VLADIMIR'S SEMINARY PRESS
575 Scarsdale Road, Yonkers, NY 10707
www.svspress.com • 1-800-204-2665

PRINTED IN THE UNITED STATES OF AMERICA

Contents

Foreword

by Metropolitan Anthony of Sourozh

'THE SPLENDOUR of God is a man fully alive.' *(St Irenaeus)* Staretz silouan was such a Man—truly, simply a Man in whom the Image of God, so badly distorted in most of us, appeared in strong relief, with great purity. A man who fulfilled his human calling in the strict, uncompromising way of Orthodox monasticism. *The Monk of Mount Athos* is not simply an account of his life by a close disciple, an attempt at conveying to us his personality and teaching—it gives us the background of traditional Orthodox spirituality which nurtured him, which indeed made him what he was, an Orthodox monk who sought to be a Man in the Image of Christ. To meet a Man is the greatest experience one can have. Reading Archimandrite Sophrony's book one can have this rare privilege. In our day when the words 'spirit' and 'charisma' are so badly misused, it is challenging to stand face to face with Staretz Silouan in whom the Spirit of God lived, moulding, teaching and enlightening him with all the sobriety, the reserve and shyness, but also the warm, outgoing love of God Himself.

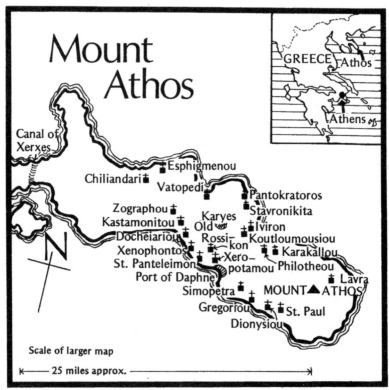

Mount
Athos

GREECE | Athos

Athens

Canal of
Xerxes

Esphigmenou

Chiliandari

Vatopedi

Pantokratoros

Zographou

Stavronikita

Karyes

Kastamonitou

Old

Iviron

Docheiariou

Rossi-

Koutloumousiou

kon

Xenophontos

Karakallou

Xero-

St. Panteleimon

potamou Philotheou

Port of Daphne

Lavra

Simopetra

MOUNT ▲ ATHOS

Gregoriou

St. Paul

Dionysiou

Scale of larger map

⊢———— 25 miles approx. ————⊣

Mount Athos is a peninsula some forty miles long and varying
between four and seven miles across. Twenty autonomous
monasteries, the first of which was founded in the year 963, share
the whole area. Many of these monasteries possess hermitages and other
dependencies, and at one time the monastic republic numbered as
many as forty thousand monks. After the first World War the
population fell sharply. When Staretz Silouan died, there were little
over three thousand monks on the 'island'. Of these some two
hundred and fifty belonged to the Russian Monastery of St
Panteleimon (which today exists with scarcely a dozen).

Orthodox monasticism comprises three degrees: the Novitiate
(during which the habit is worn though no vows have been taken); the
Lesser Schema, when the monk pronounces vows which he will renew
in a different form on being invested with the Great Schema of the
third and strictest rule.

1

Childhood and Early Years

OUTWARDLY, Blessed Staretz Silouan's life presents little of interest. Up to the time of his military service he lived like any other Russian peasant. Then came the usual period as an ordinary soldier in the army, followed by long years—forty-six in all—of the monotonous existence of a simple monk in a community. The monastery register says of him:

> '*Schema-monk* Father Silouan. Name "in the world"—Simeon Ivanovich Antonov. Peasant from the province of Tambov, district of Lebedyan, village of Shovsk. Born 1866. Professed 1896. *Schema* 1911. Performed his duties of obedience at the mill, at Kalomar, at Old Rossikon, and as steward. Died 11/24 September 1938.'

From 'born' to 'died'—how meagre the picture! Of his external life there is nothing to tell, while to touch upon a man's inner life in the sight of God may well be prying and indelicate, and to make public the depths of a Christian heart—almost sacrilege. Yet, in the belief that nothing can now dismay the Staretz, who left this world victorious over it—that nothing can now disturb his eternal rest in God—I shall try to relate something of his spiritual biography, so rich and so sublime.

The battle-ground of the spiritual struggle is, first and foremost, man's own heart; but 'the heart is deep'. The real life of the Christian is lived in this deep heart, hidden not only from alien eyes but also, in its fulness, from the owner of the heart himself. He who enters those secret recesses finds himself face to face with the mystery of being. Anyone who has ever given himself up with a pure mind to contemplation of his inward self knows how impossible it is to arrive at a complete understanding even of a few moments of his life; knows how impossible it is to detect the spiritual processes of the heart, because in its profundity the heart touches upon that state of being where there *are* no processes.

My association with Staretz Silouan being inspired by my desire to learn from him, much that would have been of interest to a biographer slipped past me unheeded. But I remember stories he told me of his life which reveal something of his interior progress and at the same time are part of his 'history'. The first of these goes back to his early childhood when he was not more than four years old. Like many Russian peasants, his father always had a welcome for wandering pilgrims. One feast-day, with especial pleasure he invited a book-pedlar to his home: he was irked by his own illiteracy and longed for knowledge. While the guest was given food and drink, young Simeon examined him with a child's curiosity, and listened attentively to his conversation. The pedlar argued that Christ was not God—indeed, that God did not exist at all. His words, 'Where *is* this God of yours, then?' particularly impressed little Simeon, who thought to himself: 'When I grow up, I shall go all over the world looking for God.' As soon as the guest had departed he said to his father, 'You make me say my prayers—but he told us there wasn't a God!' To which Simeon's father answered, 'I thought he was a wise man but he turned out to be a fool. Don't take any notice of what he said.' But the seed of uncertainty had been sown.

Years passed. Simeon grew into a sturdy lad and joined an *artel* (a group of artisans living and working together, and sharing the wages for the job) engaged on Prince Troubetskoy's estate not far from the village. His elder brother was foreman-builder, and Simeon a carpenter. The young woman who cooked for the *artel* went on a pilgrimage and visited the tomb of a remarkable early nineteenth century hermit, John Sezenov. When she returned she told them about the hermit's holy life and the miracles that took place at his tomb. Some of the older men who heard her confirmed what she said about miracles, and everyone agreed that John was a holy man.

As he listened, Simeon reflected:

'If he was a holy man, it means God is here with us, so there is no point in me going off to search the world for Him.' And at this thought his youthful heart burned with love for God. The query planted by the pedlar in the mind of the four-year-old had evidently persisted there to worry Simeon until he reached the age of nineteen, when it was resolved in so strange and apparently so naïve a manner.

After this, feeling that he had found faith, Simeon clung to the thought of God, praying much and with tears. He became aware of change in himself, and felt drawn to the monastic life, even asking his father to let him go to the great monastery at Kiev. But his father said firmly:

'Finish your military service first. Then you will be free to go.'

Simeon's unusual frame of mind lasted three months, and then he returned to his friendships with the village boys, began to walk out again with the village girls, to drink vodka, play the concertina and behave, in fact, exactly like all the other lads of the countryside.

Young, strong, handsome, and by this time prosperous too, Simeon revelled in life. He was popular in the village, being good-natured, peaceable and gay, and the village girls looked on him as a man they would like to marry. He himself was attracted by one of them and, before the question of marriage had been put, what so often happens befell late one summer evening.

Next morning, as they were working together, his father said to him quietly:

'Where were you last night, son? My heart was troubled for you.'

The mild words sank into Simeon's soul, and in later life when he recalled his father he would say:

'I have never reached my father's stature. He was quite illiterate: he even used to make a mistake in the Lord's Prayer which he had learned by listening in church. But he was a man who was gentle and wise.'

They were a large family—father, mother, five sons and two

daughters—living in affection together. The elder boys worked with their father. One Friday they were out harvesting, and it was Simeon's turn to cook the midday meal. Forgetting that it was Friday, he prepared a dish of pork for their lunch, and they all ate of it. Six months later, on a feast-day in winter, Simeon's father turned to him with a soft smile and said:

'Son, do you remember how you gave us pork to eat that Friday in the fields? I ate it but, you know, it tasted like carrion.'

'Why ever didn't you tell me at the time?'

'I didn't want to upset you, son.'

Recalling such incidents from his life at home, the Staretz would add:

'When I think of my father, I say to myself, "That is the sort of *staretz* I would like to have." He never got angry, he was always even-tempered and humble. Just think—he waited half a year for the right moment to correct me without upsetting me!'

Simeon was enormously strong, and had extraordinary powers of endurance. But this physical strength, which was later to stand him in such good stead in the accomplishment of many exceptional spiritual feats, now led to his committing his gravest sin, which afterwards he so sorely repented.

The village was celebrating the feast-day of its patron saint. It was afternoon and almost all the inhabitants were out of doors. Simeon was walking down the street with a friend, playing his concertina. Two brothers, the village cobblers, came towards him. The elder, a great burly fellow much addicted to brawling, was somewhat the worse for drink and when he drew level with Simeon he began to jeer at him, and made to snatch his concertina. Simeon managed to hand the instrument to his friend, and facing the cobbler tried to persuade him to go on his way. But the cobbler, obviously wanting to show off before the village girls who were laughingly watching the scene, went for Simeon. Here, in the Staretz' own words, is what happened next:

'At first I thought of giving in to the fellow but then I was ashamed of how the girls would laugh at me, so I hit him a great blow in the chest. His body shot away and he fell backwards with a heavy thud in the middle of the road. Froth and blood trickled from his mouth. All the onlookers were horrified. So was I. "I've killed him," I thought, and stood rooted to the spot. The cobbler's younger brother picked up a large stone and threw it at me. I twisted round but it got me in the back. I turned to him and said: "Do you want me to do the same to you?" and moved towards him but he ran away. For a long time the cobbler lay where he was. It was over half an hour before he could rise to his feet. With difficulty they got him home, where he was bad for a couple of months but luckily didn't die. For my part, I had to be on the look out for a long while: after dark, and at every corner, the cobbler's brothers and their friends would lie in wait for me with cudgels and knives, but God preserved me.'

Thus did the clamour of youth begin to drown the first summons to a monastic life of spiritual striving, but Simeon, chosen of God, was called again, this time by means of a certain vision, which followed on a period of wild living. He had dozed off and was in a light sleep, when he dreamed that he saw a snake crawl down his throat. Feeling sick with revulsion, he awoke to hear a voice saying: 'Just as you found it loathsome to swallow a snake in your dream, so I find your ways ugly to look upon.'

Simeon saw no one: he only heard the voice, unusually sweet and beautiful; but, for all its gentleness, the effect it had on him was revolutionary. He was convinced beyond doubt that he had heard the voice of the Mother of God herself, and to the end of his days he gave thanks to her for coming to raise him from his degradation.

This repetition of his original call, occurring not long before Simeon's military service, affected the whole course of his future. Renouncing the evil direction his life had taken, which he now began to hate and be ashamed of, he started to repent, and his resolve to enter a monastery, once released from the army, returned with redoubled force. A deep sense of sin awakened in him, so powerful that it radically affected not only his relations with others but his conversation too. Here

11

are some of the encounters of which I best remember hearing, which belong to this period of his life.

One day there was music and dancing in the village. Looking on, Simeon noticed a middle-aged fellow-villager playing on the concertina and dancing.

'How can you play and dance like that, Stepan?' Simeon asked him. 'Why, you once killed someone, didn't you?'

Stepan had indeed killed a man in a drunken brawl. He took Simeon on one side and replied:

'When I was serving my sentence I prayed and prayed, begging God to forgive me. And He did. That is why I can now play and be happy.'

Simeon, who not long before had himself nearly caused a man's death, knew what it was to implore God and obtain forgiveness of sins, so he could understand how it was his fellow-villager, the pardoned murderer, was at peace. (We could have no clearer illustration of the Russian peasant's precise consciousness of sin, his strong feeling of repentance and his profound religious sense.)

Another young man from Simeon's village came together with a girl from the neighbouring hamlet and got her with child. Seeing how casual was the boy's attitude, Simeon set about persuading him to marry the girl, 'because it would be a sin if you didn't'. For a long time the youth would not listen—he did not want to marry the girl. But in the end Simeon convinced him and he did so.

When the Staretz told me this story I asked him why he never married the girl he had known. He answered:

'When I wanted to become a monk I entreated God to arrange things in such a way that I might do so with an easy mind, and God heard me. While I was away soldiering a corn-chandler came to do business in our village. Seeing the girl at a village dance and noticing how gay and pretty she was and how well she sang, he fell in love with her. They lived happily together and raised a large family.'

The Staretz was fervently grateful to God for having heard his prayer. But he never forgot his sin.

Simeon did his military service at St Petersburg in a

Sappers' battalion attached to the Imperial Guard. He went off to his regiment with living faith and a deep sense of repentance, and never ceased thinking of God. He was very popular in the army, earning the reputation of being a quiet and reliable soldier; and his comrades loved him for an amiable and loyal friend.

On the eve of a certain saint's-day Simeon set out with three other young guardsmen of his company to spend the evening in town. They went into one of the big, brightly-lit taverns of the capital where a band was playing noisily. Sitting down, they ordered food and drink, and a lively conversation sprang up in which Simeon however took little part. He was so silent that one of his companions turned to him and said:

'You're not very talkative, Simeon. A penny for your thoughts!'

'I'm thinking that here we sit in a tavern, eating, drinking vodka, listening to music and enjoying ourselves, while at this very hour on Mount Athos they are in church for vespers and will be at prayer all night. And I'm wondering which of us will put up the best defence before God's Judgment Seat—them or us?'

Simeon's friend exclaimed: 'What a fellow Simeon is! We sit listening to music and enjoying ourselves, while he is on Mount Athos and at the Last Judgment!'

And the guardsman's opinion that Simeon was 'on Mount Athos and at the Last Judgment' was true not only of that particular moment but of the whole period of Simeon's military service.

There were other instances of the effects of his influence and good counsel. One day in the company's quarters he came across a soldier due for discharge who was sitting gloomily on his pallet. Simeon went up to him and said:

'What's the matter? Why do you sit there with your head in your hands instead of being glad, like everybody else, that you've done your service and are off home?'

'I've just had a letter from home,' was the soldier's reply. 'They write that my wife has had a child while I was away.' He was silent for a space. Then he shook his head, and in a low voice in which grief mingled with anger and injured pride he muttered: 'I'm scared of what I'll do to her ... That's why I don't want to go home.'

'And you,' Simeon asked him quietly, 'since you left home, how many times have you been to the house down the street?'

'Well ... ' said the soldier, as if just remembering, 'there have been times ... '

'You see, you couldn't wait. Do you think it was easy for her? It's all right for you—you're a man—but once is enough to get her into trouble. Remember what you've done. You're more in the wrong than she is. Forgive her. Go home, accept the child as your own and, you'll see, everything will be all right.'

And a few months later Simeon got a letter of thanks from the soldier, who had taken his advice.

So then, even in his early years, Simeon realised that an essential condition for peace between men is that each should have a consciousness of his own wrong-doing.

At the end of his service, not long before he was due to go home, Simeon and the company's scribe set off together to see Father John of Kronstadt, to ask for his prayers and his blessing. Not finding him at Kronstadt, they decided to leave a letter for him. The scribe wrote out in his best hand a learned epistle, full of flourishes. Simeon produced these few words: 'Batioushka,' (an affectionate diminutive of the popular word for 'father') 'I want to become a monk. Pray that the world may not hold me back.'

They returned to their barracks at St Petersburg, and on the very next day Simeon began to feel, in his own words, 'the flames of hell roaring' round him.

He went home but stayed only a week while the villagers made haste to collect linen and other gifts for him to take to the monastery. Then he said good-bye to everybody and set off for Mount Athos. But from the very day Father John of Kronstadt had prayed for him he saw 'the flames of hell' roaring round him unceasingly wherever he happened to be—in the train, at Odessa, on the boat, even in the monastery on Athos, in church, everywhere.

14

2

Arrival on Mount Athos

SIMEON reached Mount Athos in the autumn of 1892. He
entered the Russian monastery of St Panteleimon, and a life of
spiritual endeavour began.

As is the custom on the Holy Mountain, the new postulant
spent his first few days in complete quiet, recalling all his sins
and putting them down on paper to confess them. The
torments of hell through which he was passing gave birth to
ardent and profound repentance and, in no wise justifying
himself, Brother Simeon made confession of the deeds of his
whole life.

The confessor then said to him:

'You have confessed your sins before God, and you know
that they have all been forgiven. Now we will make a fresh
start ... Go in peace, and rejoice that the Lord has led you to
this haven of salvation.'

Brother Simeon's simple, faithful soul gave itself up to joy
when he heard this. Inexperienced and naïve, he had not yet
discovered that the spiritual warrior must be temperate even in
his rejoicings, and so he immediately lost the intense
concentration of effort which he had known since his visit to
Kronstadt. Now physical desire assailed him, his mind dwelt
on seductive images, and passion whispered to him to 'return
to the world and marry'.

What the young novice endured alone we do not know.
When he went to see his confessor the latter said to him:

'Do you not realise where such proposals come
from? ... You must take care never to let your mind linger on
such suggestive ideas as those, and if they come—drive them
away at once.'

His unexpected relapse deeply alarmed Brother Simeon.

Conscious now of the terrifying force of sin, he found himself once more in the midst of hell-fire and resolved to pray ceaselessly till God should have mercy upon him. Coming after the torments he had lived through, and his joy at receiving forgiveness in the sacrament of penance, this reappearance of passionate desires pierced his very soul: again he had grieved the Mother of God. He had thought that he was come to a haven of salvation, and now suddenly he saw that here, too, a man might perish.

His first 'fall' in thought made Brother Simeon soberly watchful for the rest of his life: how watchful may be judged by the fact that, from the day his confessor instructed him never to harbour impure notions, not once, during all the forty-six years of his monastic existence, did he indulge in a single carnal imagining. At this first lesson he mastered and assimilated something which many are unable to learn in long years of life, thus manifesting his true culture and wisdom, for, as the ancient Greeks said: A wise man will not err twice in the same way.

The bitterness of his remorse occasioned further conflict. Insidious thoughts now bade him 'Go into the wilderness, put on sackcloth, and work out your salvation there.'

'So be it,' replied Simeon. 'I will go and ask the Abbot for his blessing.'

'No, the Abbot will not give you his blessing.'

'First you try to send me back to the world, and now you want to drive me into the desert . . . If the Abbot will not give me his blessing it means that you are urging me to ill,' was Simeon's retort. 'And in the depths of his soul he told himself firmly: 'I will die here for my sins.'

Brother Simeon learned the spiritual life by means of a monastic rule tempered and forged through the centuries and impregnated with constant awareness of God—a rule of prayer in the solitude of the cell; long church offices; fasts and vigils; frequent confession and communion; reading, physical toil and the duties of obedience. Simple, and untroubled by the hosts of questions which assail present-day intellectuals, he adapted himself to this new way of living, like the other monks, more by an organic fusion with his surroundings than through oral lessons. The instructions of abbot, confessors and *startzy* in the monastery are in most cases brief, usually consisting of concrete directions on what to do and how to do it.

Newly-arrived postulants are taught that the Jesus Prayer—'Lord Jesus Christ, Son of God, have mercy upon me, a sinner'—is the principal prayer for the solitude of the cell. The oft-repeated invocation of the all-holy Name of Jesus delighted Brother Simeon's soul. He rejoiced to know that this prayer can be said everywhere and at all times, whatever one's work or surroundings; that it is good to 'retain' it even during church offices, and that it may take the place of such offices if one cannot be present. He prayed much and ardently, for his soul was in heavy anguish, and so he reached out with all his strength to the Saviour.

Brother Simeon spent a short while, some three weeks in all, praying the Jesus Prayer, and then, one evening as he stood before the ikon of the Mother of God, the prayer entered into his heart, to continue there, day and night, of its own accord. But not until later did he realise the sublime and rare gift he had received from the Mother of God.

Long and fervent prayer sometimes brought a measure of peace to Simeon's soul. But then there would come the sly whisper: 'You pray, and maybe you will be saved. But supposing you do not find your father or your mother in heaven, or those you love—you will have no joy there either.' Or else they suggested to him that he was leading a holy life, because his pleasant nature and punctuality in all things make him well-liked in the monastery, and he found it agreeable to be popular.

One night a strange light filled his cell, and even pierced his body so that he saw his entrails. 'Accept what you see,' came the cunning suggestion. 'It proceeds from grace.' But his soul was troubled. The prayer within him continued unceasing but the spirit of contrition had gone—to such an extent that he laughed during prayer. He hit himself a sharp blow on the forehead with his fist. Laughter stopped but still the spirit of contrition did not return and his prayer went on without it. Brother Simeon then understood that something was wrong.

After this vision of strange light devils began to appear to him and naïvely he talked to them 'as if they were people'. Their assaults gradually increased. Sometimes they said to him: 'You are holy now,' but at other times: 'You will not be saved.' Brother Simeon once asked one of these devils: 'Why do you contradict yourselves so? Sometimes your cry is that I am holy, and then you say I shall not be saved.' The devil's mocking answer was: 'We never tell the truth.'

The alternation of these diabolic insinuations—first exalting him with pride to heaven, then hurling him into the depths of eternal perdition—brought the young novice near to despair, and he prayed with the utmost intensity. Physically strong, he did not lie down to sleep but spent all his nights in prayer, either standing, or sitting on a backless stool. Only when he was worn out with fatigue did he fall asleep where he sat, for a quarter of an hour or so, and then take up his prayer again. Usually he only slept an hour-and-a-half to two hours in the twenty-four.

His first 'obedience' was to work at the monastery mill. Those were flourishing days for Russian monasticism on Mount Athos. St Panteleimon had expanded until it stood like a small city in the surrounding 'wilderness'. The number of brothers rose to almost two thousand, and from Russia visitors and worshippers came in their hundreds, many of them making a long stay in the monastery's large hostelries. All this kept the mill extremely busy. Yet Brother Simeon, who slept so little and ate so sparingly, who ceaselessly devoted himself to ardent prayer, shedding abundant and at times despairing tears, punctiliously performed the hard work he had been set, each day lifting and carrying a heavy weight of sacks of flour. (Mention may perhaps be made here of the difference between ascetic and emotional weeping which is as radical as that between heavenly wisdom and earthly wisdom. For the spiritual warrior emotional tears are an inadmissible weakness; but the other form of weeping which comes from on high and accompanies true prayer, when the mind is united with the heart, is essential if the spirit would be lifted up to God. It springs either from love of God, which softens the heart, or sorrow at separation from God. This love and this sorrow may flood a man's whole being, and so lead to 'strong crying and tears'.)

Month after month went by and the torturing assaults of the devils never slackened. Brother Simeon's strength began to fail, he was losing heart; while despair and the fear of perdition gained ground. More and more often was he possessed by the horror of hopelessness. Anyone who has gone through something of the kind knows that no mere human courage or power can hold out in this spiritual battle. Even Brother Simeon foundered and reached the final stages of desperation. Sitting in his cell before vespers, he thought to himself: 'God will not hear me!' He felt utterly forsaken. His soul plunged into the darkness of despondency. Sick at heart, he remained in this black hell for about an hour.

That same day, during vespers in the Church of the Holy Prophet Elijah (adjoining the mill), to the right of the royal gates, by the ikon of the Saviour, he saw the living Christ.

In a manner passing all understanding the Lord appeared to the young novice whose whole being filled with the fire of the grace of the Holy Spirit—that fire which the Lord brought down to earth with His coming.

There is no describing how it was with Brother Simeon at that moment. From his words and from his writings we know that a great Divine Light shone about him, that he was taken out of this world and transported in spirit to heaven, where he heard ineffable words; that he received, as it were, a new birth from on high.

The gentle gaze of the joyous, all-forgiving boundlessly-loving Christ drew Simeon's entire being to Himself, and then, departing, by the sweetness of God's love lifted his spirit to contemplation of a divinity beyond all earthly vision.

How remarkable that the simple, untutored novice should immediately have recognised both Christ appearing to him and the Holy Spirit working in him! Again and again in his writings he repeats that he knew the Lord by the Holy Spirit,

19

that he saw God in the Holy Spirit. He also used to declare that when the Lord Himself appears to the soul, the soul cannot help recognising in Him her Creator and God.

There is no denying that both the flames and torments of hell which were the prelude to Simeon's vision of Christ, and the Divine Light that shone upon him, are beyond the ken and comprehension of most people. What the spiritual man sees or hears, his emotions, his whole experience, may often seem folly, or the fruit of a psycho-pathological state, to the 'natural' man who, ignorant of the reality of the spiritual world, rejects what he does not know. Potentially, everyone is called to lead a full spiritual life. But if a man fixes his will on material things and physical satisfactions, he becomes blunted and spiritually insensitive.

Strange and incomprehensible is the mystical life of the would-be Christian! In its web of contradictions we discern assaults of evil spirits, abandonment by God, the darkness of death and the agony of hell, on the one hand; on the other, the revelation of God and the light of unoriginate being.

Words cannot compass these things.

Every human being is a unique and original phenomenon. Every ascetic's course is likewise unique and original. Simeon's unusually deep repentance makes one wonder why it is that some people repent deeply and strongly, others less deeply, and others not at all.

This is a difficult question to answer—we cannot penetrate into the mystery of the spiritual life of a man. All we are able to do is to observe certain phenomena in the inner life of a religious man, when these phenomena materialise into psychological expression. We may note certain external characteristics but we can determine nothing of the essence, since the root of each and every Christian psycho-religious fact is the absolutely unrestricted action of the Spirit of God. 'The wind bloweth where it listeth, and thou hearest the sound thereof, but canst not tell whence it cometh and whither it goeth: so is every one that is born of the Spirit.'

The second factor to escape definition is the freedom of the individual. The Christian spiritual life is made up of these two factors—the freedom of the individual and the action of God's grace.

Both faith and our repentance are to a certain inscrutable degree dependent on our freedom, as well as being gifts of God's grace. In his love God seeks man in order to give him not only life but life more abundantly. But this more abundant life is not bestowed on free man without his consent. Thus the measure of God's gift to man is subject to man's freedom, and his response, 'foreknown' by God, to the workings of grace. St Paul says: 'For whom he did foreknow, he also did predestinate to be conformed to the image of his Son.' And again, 'But when it pleased God, who separated me from my mother's womb, and called me by his grace, to reveal his Son to me . . . I conferred not with flesh and blood.'

God foreknew that Simeon, later to become *Schema-monk* Silouan, would not confer with flesh and blood but would spend his life in spiritual strivings worthy of an abundant gift, and to such a life He called him.

The thought occurs that in the person of Staretz Silouan God was giving the world a fresh example, a fresh statement, of the boundlessness of His love, in order that through him, too, men, paralysed by despair, should find new courage, as it was with St Paul: 'Howbeit for this cause I obtained mercy, that in me first Jesus Christ might shew forth all longsuffering, for a pattern to them which should hereafter believe on him to life everlasting.'

For the Staretz, Christ's commandments were not mere moral teaching. He did not debase Christianity to the level of an ethical system, as do the representatives of humanist culture who, lacking genuine religious experience, go so far as to conclude that religion is only a 'restraining power' for the ignorant, and unnecessary for themselves. For him the words of Christ meant what they meant to St Peter, who cried to his Master: 'Thou hast the words of eternal life.' He took them for spirit and life, according to the Lord's own assertion: 'The words that I speak unto you, they are spirit, and they are life.' For him the word of Christ was the life-giving Spirit, eternal life itself, God-in-action.

The light of the divine word brings sin into view.

What does the Christian understand by sin?

Sin is primarily a metaphysical phenomenon whose roots lie in the mystic depths of man's spiritual nature. The essence of sin consists not in the infringement of ethical standards but in a falling away from the divine eternal life for which man was made and to which, by his very nature, he is called.

Sin is committed first of all in the secret depths of the human spirit but its consequences distort the whole individual. A sin will reflect on a man's psychological and physical condition, on his outward appearance, on his personal destiny. Sin will, inevitably, pass beyond the boundaries of the sinner's own life to burden all humanity and thus affect the fate of the whole world. The sin of our forefather Adam was not the only sin of cosmic significance. Every sin, secret or manifest, committed by each one of us, has a bearing on the rest of the universe.

Staretz Silouan was possessed of unusual fineness of perception and astounding spiritual intuition. Even before the Lord appeared to him—and all the more so after his vision—he felt sin extraordinarily deeply and powerfully. Sin made his heart ache unendurably, and so his repentance was complete, his tears were unrestrainable, until he felt in his soul that God had forgiven him. To many this may seem strange, perhaps exaggerated, and indeed the Staretz' example is not for all men.

When repenting of sin, he did not merely seek pardon which God is swift to grant, for a single sigh of regret, maybe. He looked for a forgiveness so complete that his soul might really feel the grace of God within her again. He prayed for strength if possible never to repeat his sin. He prayed to be delivered from 'the law which is in our members'.

So then, from the beginning of time God 'foreknew' Simeon, and in a manner unknown to us gave him such a deep and potent knowledge of the essence of sin that he did actually experience the torments of hell, and from this 'lowest hell' prayed until the Lord inclined towards him and revealed Himself, making known to him, before he tasted the death of the body, the resurrection of the soul, and letting him 'see the Son of man coming in his kingdom'.

3

Monastic Strivings

BROTHER SIMEON'S vision of Christ, the most important event of his life, could not fail to bring about the most profound changes in his soul and his consciousness, and have a radical effect on his entire future development. At the moment when God appeared to him his whole being was apprised that his sins were forgiven him. The flames of hell which had roared about him vanished. The hell-like torments he had experienced during the preceding six months ceased. It was now given to him to know the peculiar joy and peace of reconciliation with God. A rare feeling of love for God and for man, for every man, flooded his soul, while his prayer of repentance and the searing, unrestrainable search for forgiveness was arrested.

During this first period after his vision Simeon's soul, which had known her own resurrection and seen the light of true and eternal being, lived in a state of paschal triumph: all was well—the world was beautiful, people were agreeable and nature was inexpressibly lovely. Strength seemed to be added to him—his body felt light and no longer a burden—and the word of God rejoiced his soul. Out of the abundance of his joy pity was born in him and he prayed for the whole world.

A little later, one feast-day morning after a night-long vigil in church, grace visited Brother Simeon a second time, as he was serving the other monks at their common meal in the refectory. But now it was less intense and afterwards its action gradually began to diminish. The memory of what he had known remained, but the peace and joy in his heart dwindled away, to be replaced by perplexity and a fear of losing what he had had. How was this loss to be avoided?

There began an attentive search in the counsels of his

confessor and the works of the ascetic Fathers for an answer to his growing bewilderment. The young monk learned that he had been granted a rare and exceptional gift but he could not understand why his mind, which had been filled with the light of the knowledge of God, was growing dark again, obsessed, despite all his efforts to keep the commandments, by those evil spirits which had disappeared after his vision of the Lord. In his perplexity he went to Old Rossikon to ask the advice of the *staretz* Father Anatol. (Old Rossikon lies in the hills to the east, about two hundred and fifty metres above sea-level and over an hour's walk from St Panteleimon. It was a quiet, desolate place which attracted those monks who wanted greater solitude for the sake of mental prayer.)

When Father Anatol had heard all the young monk was experiencing he said:

'You pray a great deal, do you?'

'Yes, I pray all the time.'

'Then I think you must be praying in the wrong way, and that is why you so often see devils.'

'I don't understand about praying in the right or the wrong way; but I do know that we must always pray, and so I pray without ceasing.'

'When you pray, keep your mind quite free from any imagining, any irrelevant thought,' said Father Anatol. 'Enclose your mind in the words of your prayer.'

Simeon stayed some time with Father Anatol who, at the end of his instructive and profitable discourse, cried out with undisguised amazement: 'If you are like this now, what will you be when you are an old man!'

Staretz Anatol was a patient and seasoned ascetic who had spent all his long life, as Staretz Silouan told me, in fasting and repentance but it was only after forty-five years in the monastery that he experienced God's great mercy and came to know the workings of grace. It was natural that he should have been astonished by the young monk but, of course, he should not have shown his amazement, and therein lay his error. Praise stimulates vanity and self-satisfaction, and stands in the way of courageous striving after perfection.

Before Simeon now lay the ascetic's battle against intrusive thoughts or suggestions from without—a battle which is no mere matter of cogitation on some abstract point but the struggle of mind and heart together against influences proceeding from entities invisible to the physical eye. Often the insidious thought comes clothed in fair words, to appear not only good but wise and even saintly. But by its effect on the heart we may recognise its origin. Only practice in guarding the mind and heart from every intrusive thought and imagining leads to understanding of the power and subtlety of demoniac insinuations. Brother Simeon's entire being was turned to God but he was still naïve and his prayer was accompanied by the imagination and so gave devils the opportunity to tempt him. The strange light which filled his cell one night and illuminated his entrails, and those monstrous figures which crowded his cell by night and even appeared by day were all pregnant with great danger. True, nearly all holy ascetics were subjected to this struggle with devils, so that to meet with them along the paths leading to spiritual perfection is a normal phenomenon, but for a simple man like Brother Simeon, brave though he was, to remain tranquil in such circumstances was impossible.

From the lives of the saints and the works of the holy ascetics, from conversations with spiritual father and others on the Holy Mountain, the young monk gradually learned to wage the ascetic war. As before, he did not lie down but slept in snatches sitting on a backless stool. He did hard physical labour all day. He practised inner obedience, setting himself to subdue his own will and learn full submission to the will of God. He was frugal in food, restrained in conversation and gesture. For long periods at a time he devoted himself to the Jesus Prayer—a feat so fraught with difficulty as to strain a man to breaking point. Yet, in spite of it all, the light of grace often left him, and hosts of devils surrounded him by night.

These alternations between a certain measure of grace followed by abandonment by God and the assaults of devils were not sterile: they kept Simeon's soul alert and vigilant. Unceasing prayer and mental watchfulness, acquired with his characteristic patience and courage, opened new horizons of spiritual knowledge and enriched him with new weapons for the war against the passions. More and more often his mind sought out that vantage-point of attention in the heart whence it could observe the inner world of the soul. By comparing his alternating states and feelings he came to a clearer understanding of what was happening to him, and grew in spiritual knowledge and judgment. He learned how insidious thoughts suggested by the different passions steal upon the soul, just as he learned to understand the workings of grace. He entered upon a life of deliberate inner striving, realising that the main purpose of such striving is the acquiring of grace. How grace is acquired and preserved, and why it forsakes the soul, became one of the supreme considerations of his life.

The mighty and incomparable experience of the holy Fathers from generation to generation has shown that only very few of all those deemed worthy of visitations of grace when they first turned to God stood fast in that spiritual struggle which must follow if the grace is to be perfect and enduring. Words cannot convey the agony of even a single night of that wrestling for grace in which Father Silouan spent so many long years. As a rule, he did not like talking about it but I remember how he once said: 'If in the beginning God had not given me to know how much He loves man, I could not have endured one of those nights. Yet they were legion.'

It was fifteen years after the Lord had appeared to him, and Father Silouan was engaged in one of those nocturnal struggles with devils which so tormented him. No matter how he tried, he could not pray with a pure mind. At last he rose from his stool, intending to bow down and worship, when he saw a gigantic devil standing in front of the ikon, waiting to be knelt to. Meanwhile the cell filled with other evil spirits. Father Silouan sat down again, and with bent head and aching heart he prayed: 'Lord, Thou seest that I desire to pray to Thee with a pure mind but the devils will not let me. Instruct me, what must I do to stop them hindering me?'

And in his soul he heard:

'The proud always suffer from devils.'

'Lord,' said Silouan, 'teach me what to do that my soul may grow humble.'

Once more, his heart heard God answer:

'Keep thy mind in hell, and despair not.'

This brief exchange marked a new and extremely important stage in Father Silouan's life. The means prescribed to him for the attaining of humility were unusual, incomprehensible, to all appearances cruel—but Father Silouan adopted them with joy and thanksgiving. His heart felt that the Lord was merciful, that the Lord Himself was guiding him. It was no new thing for him to abide in hell—he had dwelt there until his vision of the Lord. But God's direction, 'and despair not', was new. Father Silouan had reached the point of despair before; and now again, after years of onerous wrestling, after frequent periods of abandonment by God, he had been living through hours if not of actual hopelessness at least of a very similar anguish. The memory of the Lord he had seen had kept him from complete collapse but his sufferings from the loss of grace were no less grievous. Actually, what he had been experiencing was also a form of despair but despair of a different kind: in all these years, and in spite of superhuman labours, he had not attained his desire and he was losing hope. And so when he rose from his stool after wrestling for prayer and saw before him a devil expecting adoration Father Silouan felt sick at heart. It was then that the Lord Himself showed him the way to pure prayer.

What was the essence of God's prescription to Father Silouan?

It was not an abstract, intellectual disclosure but an intimation which existentially revealed to his soul that the root of all sin is pride: that God is humility and that the man who would 'put on' God must learn to be humble. Now Father Silouan realised that Christ's supreme humility, which he had experienced at the time of his vision, is an inseparable feature of Divine Love.

Now did his soul triumph—triumph after a fashion ignored by the world. It had been given to him to behold the light of eternal Being.

Father Silouan's first vision of the Lord had been full of ineffable light, and had brought him love in abundance, the joy of resurrection and an authentic impression of a transition from death to life. Why then had it withdrawn? Why had it not been a gift of irrevocable character, according to the word of the Lord: 'and your joy no man taketh from you'? Had it been intrinsically incomplete or had Silouan's soul been unable to bear it?

Now it became evident, and Silouan realised, why he had lost grace: his soul had lacked both knowledge and the strength to bear the vision. But this time he received the 'light of knowledge'. From now on he began to 'understand the scriptures', and many of the mysteries in the lives and writings of the Saints and Fathers were revealed to him.

In spirit he penetrated to the heart of the struggle of St Seraphim of Sarov who, during a time of loss of grace and abandonment by God after the Lord had appeared to him in church during the Liturgy, stood a thousand days and nights on bare stone in the wilderness, invoking God to be merciful to him, a sinner.

The real significance and force were revealed to him of what St Pimen meant when he said to his disciples, 'Be sure, children, that where Satan is, there shall I be.'

He realised that God sent St Antony to the Alexandrian cobbler to learn the same lesson—the cobbler taught him to think, 'All will be saved, only I shall be lost.'

He saw that St Sisoë was making the same reflection when he asked: 'Who can keep that thought of St Antony's always in mind? I know one man who can.' (He was referring to himself.)

Now he knew what St Makarios of Egypt meant when he said, 'Descend into thy heart and *there* do battle with Satan.' He understood what lay before those who become 'fools for Christ's sake'; and understood the paths trodden by the great ascetics Vissarion, Gerasimos of Jordan, St Arsenios and others. The road to salvation lay open to his mind's eye.

He came to know, not abstractly or theoretically but experimentally, from the experience of his own life, that the field of man's spiritual battle with evil—cosmic evil—is his own heart. He saw in spirit that sin's deepest root is pride, that scourge of humanity which has torn men away from God and plunged the world in miseries and sufferings innumerable—pride, the seed of death, which has muffled mankind in the darkness of despair.

Henceforward, Silouan was to concentrate his whole soul on acquiring the humility of Christ which had been made known to him at the time of his first vision but which he had lost. Transported in spirit into the life of the Fathers, he saw that knowledge of the path to eternal, divine life had always lain in the Church, and that by the action of the Holy Spirit this knowledge is handed down through the centuries, from generation to generation.

After this divine revelation Father Silouan stood firmly on the spiritual path. From that day his 'beloved song', as he expressed it, was:

'Soon I shall die, and my accursed soul will descend into the blackness of hell. I shall languish alone in the sombre flames, weeping for my Lord. "Where art Thou, Light of my soul? Why hast Thou forsaken me? I cannot live without Thee." '

It was not long before this brought peace of soul and pure prayer. But even so fiery a path proved far from short.

Grace no longer left him as it had before: he was conscious of it in his heart; he felt the living presence of God and was filled with wonder at the divine compassion. The deep peace of Christ visited him, and the Holy Spirit once more gave him the strength of love. But though he was less blind and foolish, though he had emerged from his long and painful struggle a wiser man and a valiant spiritual wrestler, even now he still suffered from the hesitations and inconstancies of human nature, and continued to weep with unutterable sadness when grace diminished. Another fifteen years were to pass before he received the power to repel, with a single movement of the mind (which no outward gesture betrayed), what before had so shattered him.

In proportion as the visitations of grace grew in strength and duration, so did the feeling of gratitude to God increase in Silouan's soul.

'O Lord,' he would cry, 'how can I give thanks to Thee for this new, inscrutable mercy, that Thou dost reveal Thy mysteries to the ignorant sinner that I am? The world totters in the chains of despair, while to me, the least and worst of men, Thou dost reveal eternal life. Lord, not to me alone: suffer the whole world to come to know Thee!'

Gradually, sorrow for the world ignorant of God began to dominate his prayer. Christ-like love is blessedness with which nothing in this world can compare but at the same time it is a suffering greater than any other suffering. To love with Christ's love means to drink Christ's cup, that cup which the Word Incarnate entreated the Father to let pass from Him.

The ascetic learns the great mysteries of the spirit through pure mental prayer. He descends into his inmost heart, into his natural heart first and thence into those depths that are no longer of the flesh. He thus finds his *deep* heart—reaches the profound spiritual, metaphysical core of his being; and looking into it he sees that the existence of mankind is not something alien and extraneous to him but is inextricably bound up with his own existence.

'Our brother is our life,' the Staretz often said.

Through Christ's love all men are made an inseparable part of our own individual, eternal existence. The Staretz began to understand the commandment, Love thy neighbour as thyself, as something more than an ethical imperative. In the word *as* he saw an indication, not of a required degree of love but of an *ontological community of being*—the commandment of Christ incorporates man in the whole Divine act of the creation of the world.

'The Father judgeth no man, but hath committed all judgment unto the Son . . . because he is the Son of man.'

This Son of man, Great Judge of the world, will say at the Last Judgment that 'one of the least of these' is His very Self. In other words, He assimilates every man's existence and includes it in His own personal existence. The Son of man has taken into Himself all mankind. He has accepted the 'whole Adam' and suffered for him. St Paul said that we, too, ought to think and feel like Christ—having 'the same mind which was in Christ'.

The Holy Spirit in teaching Father Silouan Christ-like love bestowed on him the gift of effectively living this love, of taking to himself the life of all humanity. The intensity of his prayer as he wept for the entire world related him and bound him with strong bonds to all mankind, to the 'whole Adam'. It was natural that having experienced his own soul's resurrection he should begin to look upon every man as his eternal brother. In this world there are various distinctions and divisions among men but in eternity we are all one. Each of us must, therefore, take heed not only for himself but for this single whole.

After his experience of the tortures of hell, and after God's prescription to him, 'Keep thy mind in hell,' it was particularly characteristic of Father Silouan to pray for the dead suffering in the hell of separation from God; but he prayed for the living, too, and for the generations to come. His prayer reached out beyond the bounds of time, and all thought of the transitory phenomena of human life, of enemies, vanished. In his distress for the world it was given to him to divide people into those who had come to know God and those who had not. He could not bear to think that anyone would languish in 'outer darkness'.

I remember a conversation between him and a certain hermit who declared with evident satisfaction:

'God will punish all atheists. They will burn in everlasting fire.'

Obviously upset, the Staretz said:

'Tell me, supposing you went to paradise and there looked down and saw somebody burning in hell-fire—would you feel happy?'

'It can't be helped. It would be their own fault,' said the hermit.

The Staretz answered him with a sorrowful countenance.

'Love could not bear that,' he said. 'We must pray for all.'

And he did, indeed, pray for all men. It became unnatural for him to pray for himself alone. All men are subject to sin, all 'come short of the glory of God'. The mere thought of this was enough to distress him—in the measure given to him he had already seen the glory of God and known what it was to come short of it. His soul was grieved by the realisation that people lived in ignorance of God and His love, and with all his strength he prayed that the Lord in His inscrutable love might give them to know Him.

To the end of his life, in spite of failing strength and illness, he kept to his habit of sleeping in snatches. This left him much time for solitary prayer, and he prayed continuously. The form of his prayer altered according to circumstance but was particularly reinforced at night, lasting till matins. This was the time when he prayed for the living and the dead, for friend and foe, for all men.

What did he think about, what did he experience, what did he say to God in those long nights of prayer for the world?

We know from some of his notes that the words of prayer should be spoken very slowly, one by one, each engrossing the whole being. The entire person focuses into a single point. The breathing changes and becomes constrained, or, to use a better term, secret, lest its 'temerity' disturb the projection and concentration of the spirit. The mind, the heart, the body to its very bones, are all drawn into this one point. Unseeing, the mind contemplates the world; unseeing, the heart lives the sufferings of the world, and in the heart itself suffering reaches its utmost limit. The heart—or, rather, the whole being—is submerged in tears.

The Staretz' prayers were not verbose, though they went on for a very long time. Indeed, prayer is often wordless, the mind in an act of intuitive synthesis being aware of everything simultaneously. During such times the soul hovers on that brink where a man may at any moment lose all sense of the world and of the body, where the mind ceases to think in separate concepts, and where the spirit will be sensible only of God. At such a moment a man forgets the world. His supplications die away, and in rapt silence he simply dwells in God.

'When the mind is entirely in God, the world is quite forgotten,' wrote the Staretz.

When, for reasons we do not know, this dwelling in God draws to a close, there in no prayer, but peace, love and profound tranquillity in the soul, and a certain intangible sadness because the Lord has left, for the soul would wish to dwell in God eternally.

The soul then lives out what is left of her contemplation.

4

Portrait of the Staretz

THE Staretz was above average height and broadly but not heavily built. He had a powerful neck and a strong body with well-proportioned limbs and workmanlike hands. Everything about his face and head was harmonious—a fine forehead, forceful chin, and gentle dark eyes, sometimes penetratingly intent and often weary from long vigil and much weeping. His beard was shaggy and frosted with white. He had the bushy eyebrows, low-set and straight, common to many thinkers; and dark hair which remained thick even in old age. (He was photographed several times but never with much success, his strong features appearing hard and sharp whereas in reality his peaceful face never gave an impression of severity.)

There were occasions, however, when the Staretz was transformed out of all recognition, when his pale countenance was lit by an expression so striking that one thought of the glory of the face of Moses, which shone so that the Israelites were afraid to look upon it.

Staretz Silouan loved the art of hesychasm and had constant recourse to it. It came to him easily because the prayer of his heart never suffered interruption from the day he received this gift from the Mother of God.

The most favourable exterior conditions for mental prayer are complete peace from sensual stimuli and, above all, darkness and quiet. The Staretz, like all hesychasts, was obliged to seek these conditions. When he was still comparatively young he persuaded the Abbot to let him go to Old Rossikon, where he built himself a small hut five minutes' walk from the community building. He was, however, soon transferred back to the monastery and appointed steward. Shutting himself in his cell, he would stow his clock away in the cupboard in order not to hear its ticking, and sometimes pull his thick woollen monastic cap over his eyes and ears. When he began to manage the storehouse outside the monastery walls he arranged for himself a private corner in the vast building where he could pursue his prayer in quiet, and he spent his nights there, going to church for matins when the monastery gates opened again. In the warehouse he caught cold after cold, and suffered much from rheumatism. During his last years illness obliged him in winter to stay in his cell in the monastery which he kept very warm. The last cell he occupied was on the same floor as the Abbot's. He frequently left it at night for another tiny room in which he stored his wood. This was on the same floor as a row of other cells that had become places for keeping wood when the number of brothers decreased. It lay in the obscure depths of a blind corridor having very thick stone walls. In this stone cell the Staretz found greater solitude and complete peace and darkness.

To the outward observer the Staretz remained an 'ordinary' man to the end of his days. He lived like all good monks—fulfilling the task given him by obedience, sober in all things, observing the monastic rule and hours. He took the Sacrament twice a week, three times during Lent; dressed simply like other working monks but was heavily clad even in summer because of his rheumatism. His work in the warehouse was easy and well within his strength, taking up comparatively little of his time though it demanded his presence all day. He was tranquil and benign to the last. He never lost his temper, nor did any earthly passion mar him inwardly or outwardly. Like all really experienced ascetics he made no show of his inner life, standing before the Father in secret, as the Lord commanded.

He was no scholar, having attended the village school for only 'two winters', but constant reading of the Scriptures and the works of the holy Fathers, and hearing them in church, had developed him considerably and made him, in the monastic sense, a well-read man. (On Mount Athos homilies from patristic literature are read aloud during the night offices, especially during the all-night vigils which last for eight or nine hours and longer.)

His lively mind was quick to grasp essentials, and long experience of spiritual struggle and inner mental prayer, together with the exceptional nature of his sufferings and the divine visitations he received, made him superhumanly wise.

Staretz Silouan had a very tender heart but his unusual sensitiveness and swift response to every kind of sorrow and affliction were quite free from sentimentality. His constant spiritual weeping never sank into querulous tears, and there was no trace of hysteria in his tireless inner striving.

Endowed as he was with a strong and powerful body, his absolute chastity is all the more astonishing. He sternly avoided any thought that might displease God, at the same time mixing freely and without constraint with all sorts of people, turning to them in love and friendship, whatever their state or manner of life—people living immoral lives arousing no disgust in him although he was sincerely distressed at their falls, just as parents are distressed at their child's misdoings.

He faced temptation with fortitude and was fearless but without any sign of self-assurance. Though afraid of nothing, he lived in awe before God: he was that rare and beautiful combination of high courage and humility.

The Staretz possessed a deep humility. He liked to honour others but to be unconsidered himself, to greet others before being greeted. He set particular store by the blessings of bishops and abbots, and indeed of all in Holy Orders, but he was never obsequious or ingratiating. He had a genuine respect for people of rank and education but no feeling of jealousy or inferiority—possibly because of his profound realisation of the transience of worldly position, wealth or even scholarship. He knew 'how greatly the Lord loveth His people,' and his love for God and man made him value and respect every man.

Simplicity stamped the Staretz' outward manner but his demeanour did not mask the aristocracy of his spirit. Even the most perceptive intuition brought into contact with Father Silouan, whatever the circumstances, would have found nothing ignoble in him: he did not know what it was to spurn or disregard. He was a stranger to affectation.

The Staretz never laughed aloud, never expressed himself equivocally, never derided or made fun of people. Occasionally a faint smile would cross his quiet, serious face but his lips did not move unless he were speaking.

Anger, as a passion, had no place in his heart yet all that was false, evil and ugly he opposed absolutely. Backbiting, pettiness, narrow-mindedness and the like found no support in him. When he encountered them he would show himself inflexible, yet contrive not to wound the man guilty of them, either by a visible reaction or an impulse of his heart (for a sensitive man would feel that, too). This he attained by inner prayer, which kept him serene and unreceptive of any evil.

Father Silouan was a man in the proper sense of the word, made in the image and likeness of God. The world is beautiful—it is the creation of a mighty God. But there is nothing more beautiful than a true man, for man is the son of God.

When I was with the Staretz my one desire was not to miss any of his spiritual teaching but to gather and assimilate into my inmost self the essence of his thought, his personality, his spirit. Talking with him was always a very simple matter. There was never any sense of constraint or embarrassment or fear of blundering, for one felt that whatever one did or said, however clumsy or even absurd, nothing would sever the contact with him or upset its peace, or meet with reproach or sharp response. The heart felt no fear in his presence and at the same time one's soul was as it were tautened in a devout effort to be worthy to breathe the spirit with which he was filled.

Coming into a fragrant place, one unconsciously expands one's chest to breathe in deeply and fill one's lungs with the fragrance. So it was in the presence of the Staretz: one's soul was possessed of a quiet, peaceful but profound longing to inhale the fragrance of that atmosphere of the spirit of Christ in which it was given him to live.

The Staretz could talk simply and humbly about things beyond the limits of normal human experience, so that if one had faith in him one could share in some degree, through one of these outwardly simple conversations, the Staretz' own supernatural state.

I remember his account of his meeting with the Russian ascetic, Father Stratonicos, who came on a visit to Athos from the Caucasus. Father Stratonicos had rare gifts of speech, prayer and tears. In the Caucasus he had raised many monks and hermits from despondency and spurred them on to fresh efforts by disclosing to them the ways of spiritual warfare. The ascetics on Mount Athos likewise received him with great love, and what he said made a deep impression on many of them. His discriminating judgment, his fine vigorous mind, his wide experience and genuine gift of prayer, all combined to make him an outstanding figure. But after nearly two months on the Holy Mountain he began to feel sorry that he had made the long and difficult journey to Mount Athos, in quest of spiritual edification, for it had apparently been in vain—he had discovered nothing new in his meetings with the monks there. He decided to go and see the father-confessor of the Russian monastery of St Panteleimon, Staretz Agathodoros, and ask him to tell him of some father with whom he could profitably discuss the question of obedience and other matters connected with monastic life. Father Agathodoros sent him to stay at Old Rossikon where at that time—it was before the First World War—there were several remarkable ascetics from the monastery.

Father Stratonicos had many conversations with the Rossikon brothers, both singly and in groups, and one feast-day one of them invited him to his cell, together with Father Silouan and several other monks. The conversation covered a wide range of subjects and all those present were carried away by what Father Stratonicos said. Father Silouan, who was the youngest there, naturally sat in a corner, saying nothing but listening attentively to the Caucasian ascetic. When the conversation was over, Father Stratonicos, who had not yet met Father Silouan alone, expressed the wish to call on him in the little hut he had built for himself five or six minutes' away from the others. It was arranged that he should come at three o'clock the next afternoon. That night Father Silouan spent in prayer, entreating the Lord to bless their meeting and discussion.

When Father Stratonicos arrived the two began talking swiftly and easily, for both of them were fixed on the same spiritual goal and their minds were wholly preoccupied by the same questions.

Listening to Father Stratonicos the day before, Father Silouan had noticed that he 'spoke from his own mind', and that what he said about the meeting of man's will with God's will, and about obedience, had been obscure.

He began the conversation by asking Father Stratonicos the answers to three questions:

'How do the perfect speak?'

'What does surrender to the will of God mean?'

'What is the essence of obedience?'

In all probability the spiritual atmosphere in which Father Silouan dwelt immediately affected Father Stratonicos. He sensed the deep significance of the questions and became thoughtful. After a long silence he said:

'I don't know. You tell me.'

Father Silouan then answered:

'The perfect never say anything of themselves ... They only say what the Spirit suffers them to say.'

At this point Father Stratonicos evidently entered into the state about which Father Silouan was speaking. A new mystery of the spiritual life which he had not known till then was disclosed to him: the mystery of the birth in the heart of the Word, proceeding from God. He saw his shortcomings in the past; he realised how far he still was from perfection—that perfection which he had sometimes thought himself to possess because of his obvious superiority over other monks (and he had been in contact with many great ascetics).

Once the first question had been resolved in the depths of his soul by his actually experiencing what Father Silouan meant, thanks to the latter's prayer, it was easy enough for him to assimilate the remaining two.

After this the two ascetics broached the subject of prayer. Father Stratonicos said that prayer without tears is not situated aright and does not come from the deep heart, and therefore bears no fruit. To this Father Silouan replied that tears, like all other bodily forces, can dry up but that a mind refined by weeping develops a certain subtle sense of God and, clear of all irrelevant thought, can then quietly contemplate Him. And this may be even more precious than tears.

Father Stratonicos went away grateful, later on returning several times to see Father Silouan; and from then on a deep love existed between them. During one of his subsequent visits he confirmed what the Staretz had said about prayer. God had evidently suffered him to know that state also.

Not long after the conversation at Old Rossikon Father Stratonicos went to see the anchorite, Father Benjamin, a man of rare nobility with a clever, erudite mind. Father Stratonicos had visited him before but this time he was unusually silent and thoughtful. Father Benjamin put some question to him, but in vain. He tried again—still no reply. At last, stretching out both arms in a gesture of surprise, he cried:

'What is wrong with you, Father Stratonicos? I don't recognise you. You were always so mettlesome but now you sit there mournfully, your inspired lips sealed. What is the matter?'

'How should I answer your questions?' replied Father Stratonicos. 'It is not good for me to speak. You have Father Silouan. Ask him.'

Father Benjamin was filled with wonder. He had known Silouan a long time, and liked and respected him; but he had never thought highly enough of him to turn to him for advice.

Once when Father Benjamin and Father Silouan were walking through the forest Father Benjamin suggested that they should both go to see Father Ambrosios, a famous *staretz* who was then confessor to the Bulgarian monastery of Zographou. Father Silouan at once agreed, and they set off. Father Benjamin wanted to know what Father Silouan would ask the *staretz*.

'I am not thinking of asking him anything just now,' said Silouan.

'Then why do you come?'

'Because you want me to.'

'Yes, but people go to see a *staretz* for the sake of edification.'

'I am subduing my will to yours, and that is of the greatest benefit to me.'

Father Benjamin was astonished. Again he did not understand.

The different branches of the complicated administration of St. Panteleimon were managed by stewards. Owing to their duties these stewards could not always fit into the general order of the monastery, and so there was a special table for them in the refectory, where each took his meals when he could. Father Silouan was a steward for many years, and on weekdays used to eat at this table.

Among the stewards was a certain monk, Father P., who was outstandingly capable, yet somehow always unlucky—his initiatives usually met with no sympathy among the fathers and his undertakings often ended in failure.

One day, after one such enterprise had resulted in disaster, he was subjected to sharp criticism at the stewards' table. Father Silouan was present but took no part in the 'prosecution'. One of the stewards, Father M., turned to him and said:

'You are silent, Father Silouan. That means you side with Father P. and are indifferent to the interests of the monastery. You don't mind the damage he has caused the community.'

Father Silouan said nothing but quickly finished eating and then went up to Father M., who by that time had also left the table.

'Father M.—how many years have you been in the monastery?'

'Thirty-five.'

'Did you ever hear me criticise anyone?'

'No.'

'Then why do you want me to begin with Father P.?'

Disconcerted, Father M. replied shamefacedly:

'Forgive me.'

'God will forgive.'

When Father Silouan was first appointed steward by the
Abbot he returned to his cell and prayed fervently that the
Lord would help him to fulfil the duties of his responsible task.
After long prayer his soul heard the answer:

'Preserve the grace given thee.'

He then understood that to preserve grace is more important
and precious than anything else, and so on entering upon his
new obedience he unwearyingly saw to it that his prayer
should not be interrupted.

There were up to two hundred workmen under his orders in
his new office. In the morning he would go round the
workshops, giving the foremen general instructions for the
day. Then he went back to his cell to weep for the 'people of
God'. His heart ached for his men and he shed tears for each
one of them.

'There's Mihail who has left his wife and children back in
their village to work here for a pittance. What must it be like
for him so far from home, away from his wife and little
children? And newly-married Nikita, who has had to leave a
pregnant wife and an old mother. As young as that, and a dear
son and husband—what must they have felt when they let him
go? There's Gregory: he left his old parents, his young wife
and two small babies, and came here to work for a crust of
bread . . . and how much does he earn? How poor they must
all be to have left their families like that! What misery must be
theirs! And the appalling poverty of every one of them! Look
at Nicky, still only a boy—what grief it must have caused his
parents to let him come so far away, to live among strangers,
for the sake of a beggar's wages! How their hearts must ache!
Oh, the poverty and suffering of the people! And all of them
like forsaken sheep—nobody cares about them, to look after

them and teach them something. No wonder they learn all manner of vice, and grow wild and rough.'

So said the Staretz to himself; and his soul suffered for all poor folk—no doubt more than they suffered themselves, for he saw in their lives what they in their ignorance did not see.

Heart speaks to heart, runs the old saying. The Staretz prayed in secret for the 'people of God' but they 'felt' and loved him. He never hung over them, never drove them hard, yet they worked better and more cheerfully for him than for anyone else. The other stewards were primarily concerned for the economic interests of the monastery and, as always happens when economic interests predominate, the individual was overlooked. The Staretz believed that the interests of the monastery, the real interests, lay in keeping Christ's commandments.

'The Lord pities all men,' he would say. And he in his turn, filled with the spirit of Christ, was sorry for all. From his vision of the world around him, his memories of the past and his profound personal experience, he lived the suffering of the people, of the whole world, and his prayer had no end. In self-forgetfulness he prayed for all the world. Pity made him want to suffer for the people. He yearned to shed his blood for their peace and salvation, and he did so in prayer.

I once asked the Staretz, 'Doesn't being steward and having to live among so many people make inner silence difficult?'

'What does inner silence mean?' he replied. 'It means ceaseless prayer, with the mind dwelling in God. Father John of Kronstadt was always surrounded by people, yet he was more with God than many solitaries.

'I became steward in an act of obedience blessed by the Abbot, so I pray better at my task than I prayed at Old Rossikon where I asked to go for the sake of inner silence. If the soul loves and pities the people, prayer is not interrupted.'

Father Silouan's attitude towards those who differed from him was characterised by a sincere desire to see what was good in them, and not to offend them in anything they held sacred. He always remained himself, convinced that 'salvation lies in Christ-like humility', and in the strength of this humility he strove with his whole soul to understand every man at his best. He found the way to the heart of everyone—to his capacity for loving Christ.

I remember a conversation he had with a certain archimandrite engaged on missionary work. Hearing from the latter's own lips how severe he was in his sermons, how harshly he pronounced judgment on other faiths, the Staretz said to him:

'Father, people feel in their souls when they are doing anything right, so that if you condemn their faith they will not listen to you. But if you were to confirm that they were really doing well, and then gently point out their mistakes and show them what they ought to put right, then they would listen to you. God is love, and therefore the preaching of His word must always proceed from love, and both preacher and listener will profit. But if you do nothing but condemn, the soul of the people will not hear, and no good will come of such preaching.

In another conversation, which took place in my presence in 1932, a monk asked the Staretz:

'What made St John Kolovos pray that his passions might return to him?' (St John Kolovos lived in the fourth century.)

To which the Staretz answered:

'By fervent repentance St John Kolovos early overcame his passions but he did not receive the gifts of love and prayer for the world. When he was left in peace his prayer grew weak, and so he started to pray for the return of his passions because in wrestling with them he dwelt in ardent, ceaseless prayer. But had he achieved prayer for the world, after overcoming the passions, he would not have needed to pray for them to tempt him anew, for I do not think a man can be in pure contemplation of God, or eager prayer for the world, and at the same time be wrestling with the passions.'

The monk then asked him:

'Why did the same *staretz* advise St Pimen the Great to allow into his heart thoughts from without and there to wrestle with them, whereas he told a less experienced brother to reject such thoughts instantly?'

Staretz Silouan replied:

athers, as this advice shows, did adopt the method
thoughts from without to enter into the heart so as
with them there; but here there are two possible
–the first when a man does not know how to
pเ๐๖-   ๒s mind, and the struggle against intrusive thoughts
begins only after they have forced their way into his heart.
This is a game at which one can lose. The second is when a
monk allows a thought to enter into his heart, not through
weakness but deliberately, in order to examine every aspect of
its action upon the mind. But neither expedient permits one to
continue in contemplation, and therefore it is better not to
admit such thoughts at all but to pray quietly with a pure
mind. Your inexperienced monk received the advice not to
enter into conversation with intrusive thoughts because he was
weak and could not have withstood a passionate thought. The
staretz' prescription was only the prelude to his learning the
difficult science of struggling against such thoughts. St Pimen,
now, was stronger and more experienced in spiritual warfare.
All the same, it is better to preserve the mind from all intrusive
thoughts and to pray with all one's soul, because the man who
prays with a pure mind receives enlightenment from the Lord.'

'How is it possible to keep the mind pure?' asked the monk.

'The holy Fathers have left us their teaching on the prayer
of the mind-in-the-heart. This prayer preserves the mind, and I
see no better means of helping a man to keep God's
commandments.'

Often young people would consult Staretz Silouan on the
way of life they should choose. Some he advised to study
theology with a view to entering the ministry. To others he
gave his blessing on the studies they had embarked on, which
he advised them to combine with prayer and monastic
temperance. Others still were advised not to pursue learning
but to devote themselves wholly to prayer and a life of
spiritual and ascetic discipline. (This last was a counsel he
very rarely gave as, in his opinion, the day was drawing near
when many erudite men would live in the world and at the
same time lead a monastic life. He thought that circumstances
in general were becoming unpropitious for the form of

monastic life that existed in ancient times but that the vocation and yearning for monasticism would always exist.)

Occasionally he spoke out with faith and definitely told his inquirer that it was God's will for him to do this or that. At other times he answered that he did not know what God's will for him was. He would declare that the Lord sometimes did not reveal His will even to the Saints, because the man who had sought out the saint had done so with a false and deceitful heart.

The Staretz was utterly convinced that the spiritual life—that is, the ascetic life of prayer and profound faith—was higher than every other way, and that the man to whom it had been given should for its sake set aside all else, even learning. (Incidentally, he believed that if the spiritual man were to abandon the spiritual life and turn his mind to learning, he would show greater capacities as a scholar than the man less talented spiritually. In other words, that the man with mystical gifts, living the life of the spirit, lives on a higher, nobler plane than the man whose province is learning in the sphere of logical thought; and since the spiritual man has a higher form of existence, he will, on descending to a lower plane, show greater talent there, though perhaps not immediately, than the non-spiritual person. The Staretz said that 'the children of this world are in their generation wiser than the children of light' not because they are wiser in actual fact but because 'the spiritual man is absorbed by God and has little time to spare for the things of the world'.)

One year on his feast-day I went to see Father Diadochos, who had charge of the monastery's big sewing-workshop, and found him talking with some of his spiritual friends, a father-confessor, Father Trophimos and Staretz Silouan. The father-confessor was relating something he had read in the newspapers and, turning to Staretz Silouan, he asked:

'What do you think, Father Silouan?'

'*Batioushka,* I don't like newspapers with their news.'

'Why not?'

'Because the reading of newspapers darkens the mind and hinders pure prayer.'

'How odd,' said the father-confessor. 'For my part I find just the contrary: newspapers help me to pray. We live here in the wilderness, seeing nothing, and gradually the soul forgets the world and becomes shut up in herself. Prayer then grows weak. But when I read the newspapers I see how it is with the world, how people suffer, and that makes me want to pray. Then, whether celebrating the Liturgy or praying in my own cell, I entreat God for all mankind, for the whole world.'

'When the soul prays for the world,' said Father Silouan, 'she knows better without newspapers how the whole earth is afflicted and what people's needs are. She can pity men without the help of papers.'

'How can the soul know of herself what goes on in the world?'

'Newspapers don't write about people but about events, and then not the truth. They confuse the mind and, whatever you do, you won't get at the truth by reading them; whereas prayer cleanses the mind and gives it a better vision of things.'

'I don't quite see,' said the father-confessor.

We all waited for Staretz Silouan to reply but the Staretz sat on in silence, head bent, not suffering himself to explain in the presence of a father-confessor and older monks how the soul can, in spirit, know the life of the world and the needs and tribulations of men when, remote from all things, she prays for the universe.

Father Silouan, who was deemed worthy of knowledge which is granted to very few, was too unassuming to do more in general conversation than give an intimation of what he thought; and because of this his great wisdom and quite exceptional experience often escaped the notice of those who talked with him. When he saw that his interlocutor did not accept his first words the Staretz usually made no attempt to 'explain' things which are first and foremost the fruit of experience—and his spiritual reticence would not permit him to disclose his experience. Thus during his lifetime he remained 'unrecognised'. There is no doubt that this was not only God's will for him but his own desire, too, which God accepted and fulfilled, concealing him even from the monks of the Holy Mountain. Yet not altogether—Staretz Silouan did not remain utterly hidden: there were monks and others (visitors to Athos or people who corresponded with him) who esteemed and loved him deeply, among them bishops and theologians as well as pious laymen.

I remember a certain Orthodox foreigner who made a fairly long stay in the monastery. The Staretz created a deep impression on him. One day, meeting the foreigner in a corridor of the monastery, Father N of the Council of *Startzy,* who was one of the most influential members of the community, said to the visitor:

'I can't understand how a scholar like you can take pleasure in going to see Father Silouan, an illiterate peasant. Haven't we anybody cleverer than that?'

'It needs a "scholar" to understand Father Silouan,' was the reply.

Why scholars revered and went to see Staretz Silouan remained a mystery to this same Father N, and in conversation with Father Methodios, who ran the monastery bookshop for many years, he remarked:

'I wonder why they go to him. After all, he reads nothing.'

'He reads nothing but fulfils everything, while others read a lot and perform nothing,' was Father Methodios' comment.

5

The Staretz' Doctrinal Teaching

IN reality Staretz Silouan pronounced no doctrinal teaching. What follows is an attempt to formulate the things he told me over the years. When I turned to him with questions, or listened to him, I recognised that he spoke out of an experience granted from on high, and I looked upon his words to a certain extent as the Christian world looks upon the holy Scriptures which impart truths as acknowledged and certain facts. What the Staretz said was not the fruit of the workings of his own brain: it expressed actual experience and existential knowledge, and was therefore a positive testimony to the realities of spiritual being. The search for logical proofs was alien and superfluous in his eyes, and as irrelevant as for the Scriptures. Like St John the Divine he would say: 'We know.' Take the following from his writings:

'We know that the greater the love, the greater the sufferings of the soul. The fuller the love, the fuller the knowledge [of God]. The more ardent the love, the more fervent the prayer. The more perfect the love, the holier the life.'

Each of these four propositions might have been the precious culmination of complex philosophical, psychological and theological arguments but the Staretz had no need of such arguments and did not descend to them.

In his conversations, simple as was their form, Father Silouan seemed able, by the strength of his prayer, to transport his interlocutor into a special world. The man talking with him was introduced into that world not theoretically but actually, by an inner experience transmitted to him. True, so far as I know, hardly anybody was afterwards able to live out in his own life what had thus been made known to him in conversation with the Staretz. Many who had run eagerly to him for guidance afterwards fell away because they found themselves unable to live in accordance with what he said. His counsel was simple, quiet and kind; but to follow it one has to be as unsparing of self as was the Staretz. The firmness of purpose is required which the Lord demands from His followers—a resoluteness amounting to self-hatred.

Discovering the Will of God

The Staretz used to say, 'It is good at all times and in all things to ask God for understanding of what to do or say, and in what manner.' In other words, on every separate occasion we should seek to discover God's will and the way to perform it.

The quest to know God's will is the most important thing in a man's life, since when he happens on the path of the will of God he becomes incorporate with divine, eternal life.

There are various ways of acquiring this knowledge of God's will. One is through the word of God—through the commandments of Christ. But the Gospel commandments express the will of God in its over-all, ultimate sense, whereas man in his everyday life is confronted with an endless complexity of situations, and very often does not see what to do to comply with God's will.

The man who has the love of God in his heart, prompted by this love, acts in accordance with dictates which approximate to the will of God. But they only approximate: they are not perfect. The unattainableness of perfection obliges us all continually to turn to God in prayer for understanding and help.

Not only perfect love but complete knowledge is out of our reach. An act performed, it would seem, with the very best intention often has undesirable and even evil consequences because the means employed were bad, or simply mistaken. People are often heard to justify themselves by saying that their intentions were good. But good intentions are not enough. Life abounds with mistakes of this kind. That is why the man who loves God never ceases to ask Him for understanding, and has a constant ear for the sound of His voice.

In practice, the process is as follows: every Christian, and in particular every bishop or priest, when faced with the necessity of finding a solution consonant with the will of God, makes an inner rejection of all his own knowledge, his preconceived thoughts, desires and plans. Freed from everything 'of his own', he then turns his heart to God in prayer and attention, and the first thought that finds birth in his soul after such prayer he accepts as a sign from on high. Such search for the knowledge of God's will through direct invocation in prayer leads man, especially in need and distress, 'to hear God answering him in his heart,' as the Staretz said, 'and he learns to understand God's guidance.'

The man who adopts this course will succeed only if he has come to know by experience how the grace of the Holy Spirit works. Then the real significance of Father Silouan's question to Father Stratonicos—'How do the perfect speak?'—will be disclosed to him. The words of the Apostles and holy Fathers, 'It seemed good to the Holy Ghost, and to us,' will sound natural. He will better understand the passages in the Old and New Testaments which tell of similar direct conversations between the soul and God, and he will have a truer conception of the manner in which the Apostles and Prophets spoke.

Man is created in God's image and likeness and is called to the fulness of direct communion with God. All men, therefore, without exception, should be treading this way, but in fact experience shows that it is by no means a path for everyone. This is because most people neither hear nor understand 'God speaking in their hearts: they listen to the urging of passion which inhabits the soul and with its clamour drowns the still small voice of God.

In the Church another course lies open to us: to seek out and obey the counsels of a spiritual father. This is what the Staretz himself did, considering the humble path of obedience to be the most trustworthy of all. And I remember he thought that on the psychological plane, too, it was not difficult to see the advantage of obedience to a spiritual father. He used to say that when a father-confessor answers a question in the performance of his ministry he is at that moment untouched by the passion influencing his inquirer, and so he can see more clearly and is more easily accessible to the action of God's grace. His answer will usually bear the imprint of imperfection, but this is not because he lacks the grace of knowledge but because perfection is beyond the strength and grasp of the man inquiring of him.

When asked for advice a spiritual father prays to God for understanding. But he answers in his capacity as man, according to the measure of his faith. 'I believe, and therefore have I spoken,' wrote St Paul, but 'we know in part, and we prophesy in part.' When a spiritual father gives advice, or tells a man what to do, he himself is anxious not to sin and is on trial before God. The moment, then, that he meets with an objection, or even an inner resistance, on the part of his questioner, he does not insist, nor does he presume to affirm that what he was saying was the expression of God's will. In his capacity as man, he withdraws.

Why? On the one hand because the Spirit of God suffers neither violence nor argument; on the other because the will of God is too mighty to be contained or receive perfect expression in human words. Only the man who accepts these words of his spiritual father with faith as being pleasing to God, who does not submit them to his own judgment, or argue about them, has found the true way, for he genuinely believes that 'with God all things are possible'.

On Obedience

The Staretz attributed the utmost importance to the question of obedience, not only for monks and Christians individually but in the life of the whole 'body of the Church'. Inner obedience to abbot and spiritual father he looked upon as a sacrament of the Church and a gift of grace. He would accept his confessor's first words, his first intimation, and carry the conversation no further. This is the wisdom and mystery of true obedience, the purpose of which is to know and fulfil God's will, and not man's.

Many people make the mistake of looking upon a spiritual guide as just as ordinary man like themselves, having like failings. (They think they must 'explain all the circumstances to him, otherwise he won't understand'. He may easily 'make a mistake' and must, therefore, be 'put on the right track'.) But those who contradict and correct their spiritual father place themselves above him and are no longer disciples. True, nobody is perfect, and there is no man who would venture to teach like Christ, 'as one having authority', for the teaching is 'not of man' and 'not after man'.

In the vast sea which is the life of the Church the true tradition of the Spirit flows like a thin pure stream, and he who would be in this stream must renounce argument. When anything of self is introduced the waters no longer run clear, for God's supreme wisdom and truth are the opposite of human wisdom and truth. Such renunciation appears intolerable, insane even, to the self-willed. But the man who is not afraid to 'become a fool' has found true life and true wisdom.

Concerning Tradition and the Scriptures

The Staretz' regard for obedience as an essential condition for discovering God's will is closely linked with his attitude towards Sacred Tradition and the Word of God. The living tradition of the Church, continuing down the centuries from generation to generation, is one of the most material and at the same time most subtle facets of her life. When there is any resistance, however slight, on the part of a disciple the thread of pure tradition is broken and the teacher silenced.

For the Staretz the life of the Church meant life in the Holy Spirit, and Sacred Tradition the unceasing action of the Holy Spirit in her. Sacred Tradition, as the eternal and immutable dwelling of the Holy Spirit in the Church, lies at the very root of her being, and so encompasses her life that even the Scriptures themselves come to be but one of its forms. Thus, were the Church to be deprived of Tradition she would cease to be what she is, for the ministry of the New Testament is the ministry of the Spirit 'written not with ink, but with the Spirit of the living God; not in tables of stone, but in fleshy tables of the heart'.

Suppose that for some reason the Church were to be bereft of all her liturgical books, of the Old and New Testaments, the works of the holy Fathers—what would happen? Sacred Tradition would restore the Scriptures, not word for word, perhaps—the verbal form might be different—but in essence the new Scriptures would be the expression of that same 'faith which was once delivered unto the saints'. They would be the expression of the one and only Holy Spirit continuously active in the Church, her foundation and her very substance.

If St Paul had 'the mind of Christ', how much more does this apply to the whole Body of which St Paul is one member! If the writings of St Paul and the other Apostles are Holy Scripture the new Scriptures of the Church, written, as we have supposed, after the loss of her books, would in their turn become Holy Scripture, for according to the Lord's promise the Holy Trinity, Father, Son and Holy Spirit, will be in the Church even unto the end of the world.

Men are wrong when they set aside Sacred Tradition and go, as they think, to its source—to the Holy Scriptures. The Church has her origins not in the Scriptures but in Sacred Tradition. The Church did not possess the New Testament during the first decades of her history. She lived then by Tradition only—the Tradition St Paul calls upon the faithful to hold.

Unwavering faith in the veracity of the Church's teaching and a deep trust in all that the Church has recognised and confirmed in her experience lie at the basis of the Athonite monk's life, preserving him from dilettantism and fumbling research. This faith makes him the co-possessor of the universal Church's boundless riches and immediately gives an absolutely authentic character to his own personal experience.

Each new book with claims to inclusion in the teaching of the Church is considered from every aspect and especially with regard to the influence it may have on the lives of men.

This last test is extremely important because of the close connection between dogmatic teaching and life. The Church accepts nothing contrary to or inconsistent with the spirit of the love of Christ by which she lives. And I believe that in his writings blessed Father Silouan has provided us with the latest and most trustworthy criterion of truth in the Church: Christ-like love for enemies, and Christ-like humility.

The Staretz held theology and theologians in great respect but the merits of scientific theology and its positive rôle related in his mind exclusively to the historical aspect of Church life and not to the real, eternal life of the Spirit.

There is a certain inevitable inconstancy and lack of precision inherent in human language, which persists even in Holy Scripture, so that expression of Divine Truth in terms of human language is only possible within set limits. The Staretz believed that the way to apprehend the Word of God lay in the fulfilment of Christ's commandments. This was the Lord's own teaching.

'And the Jews marvelled, saying, How knoweth this man letters, having never learned? Jesus answered them, and said, My doctrine is not mine, but his that sent me. If any man will do his will, he shall know of the doctrine, whether it be of God, or whether I speak of myself.'

The Lord summed up the whole of Holy Scripture in one short saying: 'Love God and thy neighbour.' Yet the meaning of Christ's word *love* will remain a mystery for the philologist to all eternity. The word *love* is the very name of God, and its true sense is only revealed by the action of God Himself.

Man in the Likeness of Christ

The Staretz often both said and wrote that those who keep the Lord's commandments are in the likeness of Christ. This likeness to Christ may be on a larger or smaller scale, but there are no limits to it.

'The Lord so loved His creature,' he would say, 'that man is in the likeness of God.' (He had in mind the words of St John the Divine: 'We shall be like him; for we shall see him as he is.')

The Staretz was deeply attached to the saying of Christ:

'Father, I will that they also, whom thou hast given me, be with me where I am; that they may behold my glory.'

To behold this glory without participating in it is impossible, and so the words 'that they may behold my glory' mean 'that they, too, may be given this glory'.

God is Love, and as infinite love He would give the whole of Himself to man. 'The glory which thou gavest me I have given them.' And when this glory is given to him, although by his nature he continues unalterably a created thing, by the content and compass of his being man verily becomes a god, in the same measure as Christ Himself, Son of God, 'sitting in the throne of the Father'.

Just as the Word, co-Eternal with the Father, in the act of Incarnation took the form of human being and became man, so man in Christ assumes the form of Divine Being in all its infinity, even to identity with the Creator in the Act of Being. It is to this that we are called by Christ: 'Be ye therefore perfect, even as your Father which is in heaven is perfect.'

In his recognition of the Lord as the closest, most precious, most fatherly of Fathers, the Staretz used to say, 'The Holy Spirit has made us His kin.'

By His coming into the soul the Holy Spirit makes man kin with God, so that in a mighty sweep of conviction the soul addresses the Lord as 'Father'.

Concerning our Relations to our Neighbour

We see in others that which our own spiritual experience has shown us about ourselves, and so a man's attitude to his fellow is a sure sign of the degree of self-knowledge he has attained. Whoever has experienced the deep and intense suffering of the human spirit when excluded from the light of true being, and, on the other hand, knows what it is to be in God, has no doubt that every human being is a permanent eternal value, more precious than all the rest of the world. He is conscious of man's worth, conscious that 'the least of these my brethren' is dear in God's sight, and so he will never think of murdering, harming or even giving offence to his neighbour.

The man who merely 'believes', the man with only a moderate personal experience of grace and a still vague sense of the reality of eternal life, will in the measure of his love for God keep himself from sin; but his love will be far from perfect and may not prevent him from hurting his brother.

But the man who pitilessly, for his own benefit and interest, harms another, who plots or commits bloodshed, has either become like a wild animal and acknowledges in his depths that he is a brute being—which means that he does not believe in eternal life—or has set his feet on the path of demoniac spirituality.

His vision of Christ gave the Staretz to experience man's godlike state. He hailed all men as bearers of the Holy Spirit, of that Light of Truth which to some degree inhabits and enlightens every man. The man who knows this Light beholds it in others.

Unity of the Spiritual World and the Greatness of the Saints

The life of the spiritual world the Staretz recognised as one life, and because of this unity every spiritual phenomenon inevitably reflects on the state of the whole world: if the phenomenon be good 'all heaven' rejoices; if evil 'all heaven' sorrows. Though every spiritual phenomenon inevitably leaves its mark on the entire world, that intangible communion in the existence of all things of which the Staretz wrote is chiefly peculiar to the Saints. Such awareness as this, which exceeds the bounds of human knowledge, he ascribed to the action of the Holy Spirit in whom the soul 'sees' and embraces the whole world in her love. The Saints partially receive this gift through the Holy Spirit while they are still on earth, but it increases when they pass away.

Spiritual Vision of the World

The Staretz frequently said that 'when the mind is in God the world is forgotten,' and he also wrote: 'The spiritual man soars like an eagle in the heights, and with his soul feels God, and beholds the whole world, though his prayer be in the darkness of the night.'

Is there not some contradiction here? Is not this vision of the world mere imagination? But again he wrote: 'Rare are the souls that know Thee; with but few is it possible to speak of Thee.'

What he taught was that pure prayer draws the mind into the innermost depths of the heart and there gathers the whole man, even his body, into one. With the mind thus submerged in the heart all earthly images are set aside and the soul, straining towards God in inner prayer, in the light proceeding from God sees herself after a quite particular fashion. She sees, not external phenomena or circumstances, but herself stripped bare, her profundities unveiled.

But though this form of contemplation takes note of no external factor, being gathered up into a point and totally directed towards the source of life, towards God, in it are revealed the bounds between which the whole created spiritual world moves and has its being, and the soul, detached from everything and seeing nothing, in God beholds the entire world and knows that she is one with this world, as she prays for it.

'I want only one thing: to pray for all men as for myself,' wrote the Staretz.

Two Ways of Acquiring Knowledge of the World

The Staretz had a lively, attractive and unusually adventurous intelligence.

'With our minds,' he writes, 'we cannot come to know even how the sun was made; and if we beg God to tell us how He made the sun, the answer rings clear in our soul: "Humble thyself and thou shalt know not only the sun but the Creator of the sun." '

These almost naïve words refer to two different forms of knowledge of being. The usual way to acquire knowledge, the one we all know, consists in the directing of the intellectual faculty outwards where it meets with phenomena, sights, forms, in innumerable variety—a differentiation *ad infinitum* of all that happens. This means that the knowledge thus acquired is never complete and has no real unity. Insistently seeking unity, the mind is forced to take refuge in synthesis, which cannot help being artificial. The unity arrived at in this way does not really and objectively exist. It is merely a form of abstract thinking natural to the mind.

The other way to acquire knowledge of being is to turn the spirit in and towards itself and then to God. Here the process is the exact reverse. The mind turns away from the endless plurality and fragmentariness of the world's phenomena, and with all its strength addresses itself to God in prayer, and through prayer is directly incorporated in the very act of Divine Life, and begins to see both itself and the whole world.

To obtain knowledge after the first manner is natural to man in his fallen state. The second is the way of the Son of man.

'The Son can do nothing of himself, but what he seeth the Father do . . . For the Father loveth the Son, and sheweth him all things that himself doeth . . . For as the Father hath life in himself; so hath he given to the Son to have life in himself.'

How ingenuous those who hope to attain perfection and fulness of knowledge by means of experimental science!

Now the beginning of the second manner of obtaining knowledge is pure prayer and the gift of performing miracles. Inserting themselves in the current of the will of the Father, the Saints, like the Son of God, performed miracles, and thus became partakers and labourers together with God in the Act of the creation of the world. Within the confines of earthly life experience of this kind of knowledge is always incomplete, but after they have left this world those who are growing to God become associates in divine omniscience and omnipotence.

The Way of the Church

'It is given to our Church through the Holy Spirit to understand the mysteries of God, and she is strong in the holiness of her thought and in her patience.' *(Staretz Silouan)*

The mystery of God which the Church understands in the Holy Spirit is the love of Christ.

The hallowed thought of the Church is that all men should be saved. The path she follows towards this end is the path of patience, that is, of sacrifice.

In preaching the love of Christ to the world, the Church calls all men to the fulness of divine life but many do not understand her call, and repudiate it. When she bids men keep Christ's commandment and love their enemies the Church finds herself caught between conflicting forces who naturally vent their anger upon her when she crosses their course. But the Church, actualising Christ's mission on earth—the salvation of the whole world—purposely takes upon herself the burden of the world's anger, just as Christ took upon Himself the sins of the world. And as Christ was persecuted in this world of sin, and had to suffer, so the true Church of Christ must be persecuted and suffer, too. The Lord Himself and the Apostles spoke of this spiritual law of life in Christ, and St Paul gave it categorical expression when he wrote: 'Yea, and all that will live godly in Christ Jesus shall suffer persecution.'

'Blessed are the peacemakers: for they shall be called the children of God.'

What the Lord says here is that those who preach the peace of God shall be like Him, the Only-Begotten Son of God—like Him not only in His glory and resurrection but also in His humiliation and death.

Distinguishing Good from Evil

The Staretz likewise held that the certain sign by which to recognise good from evil is not so much the end, which may appear to be holy and sublime, as the means selected to achieve the end.

God alone is absolute. Evil, which has no original essence but is merely the resistance of the free creature of God, cannot be absolute. Therefore evil does not and cannot exist of itself but must live like a parasite on the body of good. Evil must find a justification, must appear disguised as good, and often the highest good. Evil always and inevitably contains an element appearing to have a positive value, and it is this which seduces man. Evil strives to present its positive facet as a jewel so precious, or at all events so desirable, that all means are justified to attain it.

Absolute good cannot be achieved in man's earthly existence: there is an element of imperfection in all human undertakings. This presence of imperfection in human good on the one hand, and the inevitable presence of some pretence of good in evil on the other, often make it extremely difficult to distinguish good from evil.

The Staretz believed that evil always proceeds by means of deceit, camouflaging itself as good, whereas good in order to realise itself does not need the co-operation of evil. Therefore as soon as wrong means—malice, lying, violence and the like—make their appearance one is entering a domain alien to the spirit of Christ. Good is not attained by evil means and the end does not justify the means. *Good not obtained by good means is not good.* This is the testament we have received from the Apostles and holy Fathers. Although good frequently triumphs and by its appearance rectifies evil this does not mean that evil has led to good, that good has come out of evil. That is impossible. But the power of God is such that, where it appears, it heals all things so wholly that no scar remains—the damage caused by evil is effaced—for God is the fulness of life and creates life from nothing.

On the Difference between Christian Love and the Justice of Men

Men usually interpret justice in terms of legal responsibility. We reject the idea of laying one man's guilt on another, as not according with our conceptions of equity. But the spirit of the love of Christ speaks otherwise, seeing nothing strange but, rather, something entirely natural, in sharing the guilt of those we love, and even in assuming full responsibility for their wrongdoing. Indeed, it is only in this bearing of another's guilt that the truth of love is revealed and grows to full awareness of itself.

Many of us cannot, or do not want to, accept and suffer of our own free will the consequences of Adam's original sin. 'Adam and Eve ate the forbidden fruit—but what has that to do with me?' we protest. 'I am ready to answer for my own sins but certainly not for the sins of others.' And we do not realise that in arguing thus we are repeating within ourselves the sin of Adam, making it our own personal sin, leading to our own personal fall. Adam denied responsibility, laying all the blame on Eve and on God who had given him this wife; and by so doing he destroyed the unity of Man and his oneness with God. Each time we refuse to take on ourselves the blame for the common evil, for the deeds of our neighbour, we are repeating the same sin and likewise shattering the unity of Man. The Lord questioned Adam before Eve, and we must suppose that if Adam had not justified himself but had taken upon his shoulders the responsibility for their common sin the destinies of the world might have been different, just as they will alter now if we in our day assume the burden of the transgressions of our fellow men.

We can all find ways of justifying ourselves on all occasions but if we really examine our hearts we shall see that in justifying ourselves we are not guileless. Man justifies himself firstly because he does not want to acknowledge that he is even partially guilty of the evil of the world, and secondly because he does not realise that he is gifted with godlike freedom—he sees himself merely as part of the world's phenomena and, as such, dependent on the world. There is a considerable element of bondage in this, and self-justification, therefore, is a slavish business unworthy of a son of God.

I saw no tendency towards self-justification in the Staretz. But it is strange—so different are the conceptions of the sons of the Spirit of Christ from those of the world—how to many people this taking the blame for the faults of others savours of subjection. They cannot believe that it is possible to feel all humanity as a single whole to be incorporated in the personal existence of every man. According to the second commandment, *Love thy neighbour as thyself,* each of us must and can comprise all mankind in his own personal being, in the same way as each of the three Persons of the Godhead contains the fulness of Divine Being. Thus we shall accept all the evil in the world not as something extraneous but as evil in which we, too, have our part, and contend with evil, with cosmic evil, beginning in our own selves.

The Staretz himself always spoke only of the love of God and never of His justice, but I purposely got him to talk about this, and here approximately is what he said:

'One cannot say that God is unjust—that there is injustice in Him—but neither can one say that He is just in our sense of the word. St Isaak of Syria wrote: *'Do not presume to call God just: for what sort of justice is this—we sinned, yet He gave up His Only-Begotten Son on the cross?'* To which we could add: 'We sinned, yet God set His holy angels to serve our salvation. But the angels, filled with love as they are, themselves desire to wait upon us and so accept affliction in our service. The Lord surrendered the animals and the rest of the created world to the law of corruption because it was not proper for them to remain immune when man, for whose sake they were created, through his own sin became the bondsman of corruption. So, in part willing, in part perforce, "the whole creation groaneth and travaileth in pain together until now," in sympathy with men.'

The love of Christ being a divine force and a gift of the Holy Spirit, the One Spirit acting universally, makes all men ontologically one. Love takes to itself the life of the loved one. The man who loves God is drawn into the life of the Godhead; he who loves his brother draws his brother's life into this own hypostatic being; the man who loves the whole world in spirit will embrace the whole world.

On Freedom

The Staretz' life was spent, above all, in prayer, and the praying mind does not think—does not reason—but lives. Its activity does not consist in the manipulation of abstract concepts but in participation in being. The truly praying mind has to do with categories different in quality from those of rational reflection. It is concerned not with intellectual categories but with actual existence, an existence which cannot be included within the narrow framework of human concepts.

The Staretz was not a philosopher in the usual sense of the word: he was a sage, and knew things beyond the bounds of philosophy. He would pray:

'Lord, people have forgotten Thee, their Creator, and they seek their own freedom. They do not understand that Thou art merciful and lovest the repenting sinner, and givest him the grace of Thy Holy Spirit.'

He used few words in his prayer to the omniscient God and did not amplify his thought. 'Men seek their own freedom,' that is to say, freedom outside God, outside true life, in 'outer darkness', where there is and can be no freedom, for freedom can only exist where there is no death, where there is authentic eternal existence—that is, in God.

'Thou are merciful and dost give them the grace of the Holy Spirit,' and man then becomes free. 'Where the Spirit of the Lord is, there is liberty.' 'Whosoever committeth sin is the servant of sin. And the servant abideth not in the house for ever: but the Son abideth ever. If the Son therefore shall make you free, ye shall be free indeed.'

Existential or, as the Staretz called it, experienced knowledge of human liberty is extraordinarily profound in the prayer of grace. Father Silouan recognised with his whole soul that there is only one real servitude—the servitude of sin—and one real freedom, which is resurrection in God.

Until man attains his resurrection in Christ everything in him is disfigured by fear of death and, consequently, by the servitude of sin, too; while of those who have not yet come to know the grace of the resurrection only the 'blessed . . . that have not seen and yet have believed' escape such disfiguring.

God is not envious. God has no self-esteem, no ambition. Infinitely great, He is likewise infinitely humble. Divine humility differs from our human humility in that it never involves comparison: it is an inalienable attribute of the boundlessly generous love of God. God patiently seeks out each one of us along our way, and therefore we can all in varying degrees come to know God. But perfect knowledge of God is not possible apart from or without Christ—no man knoweth' the Father 'save the Son, and he to whomsoever the Son will reveal him'.

Without Christ no mystical experience can lead to knowledge of Divine Being as One inscrutable, absolute Objectivity in Three inscrutable absolute Subjects—the Trinity consubstantial and undivided. In Christ, however, this revelation, this knowledge becomes the light of eternal life streaming down on every manifestation of our existence.

Staretz Silouan testified categorically that the Divinity of Jesus Christ cannot be known otherwise than by the Holy Spirit. And this knowledge is in itself eternal life, since it is inspired by God's action in us.

Dogmatic consciousness understood as *knowledge* of God is conferred by God Himself. It certainly does not always find expression in the spoken or written word. When God in His Providence descends to a soul, no desire is felt to interpret logically to others or, indeed, even to oneself the experience of communion with God. The whole being is given over without the slightest resistance or reserve to the action of God the Holy Spirit. No distance then separates God from man. Thus the experience feels absolutely and uniquely natural, and the soul emerges convinced that her former state was a sub-natural one.

I know of no terms in which to describe the spiritual life, incomprehensible and indefinable in its sources, simple and unique in its essence. Some people might call it the domain of the super-conscious but this word is unintelligible and defines nothing more than the correlation between the reflex consciousness and the world beyond its bounds.

If we move from this indefinable domain into the sphere within the competence of our inner observation and which is even to a certain extent amenable to verification, the spiritual life manifests itself in two ways: as a spiritual state or experience, and as a dogmatic consciousness. These two aspects, distinct and separate from each other in their 'incarnation'—in the formula in which they are clothed in our empirical life—in their essence are one and indivisible. This means that every ascetic act, every spiritual state, is indissolubly linked to a corresponding doctrinal cognition.

With this connection in mind, I always looked for the doctrinal consciousness to which the Staretz' mighty prayer and weeping for the world were tied; and now I would essay an expression of this doctrinal consciousness of his in language more comprehensible perhaps to the contemporary reader than are the Staretz' own words in their holy simplicity.

The Staretz both said and wrote that Christ-like love cannot suffer any man to perish, and in its care for the salvation of all men walks the way of Calvary.

'The Lord gives the monk the love of the Holy Spirit, and by virtue of this love the monk's heart sorrows over the people because not all men are working out their salvation. The Lord Himself so grieved over the people that He gave Himself to death on the cross. And the Mother of God bore in her heart a like sorrow for men. And she, like her beloved Son, desired with her whole being the salvation of all. The same Holy Spirit the Lord gave to the Apostles, to our holy Fathers and to the pastors of the Church.'

In the really Christian sense the work of salvation can only be done through love—by attracting people. There is no place for any kind of compulsion. In seeking the salvation of all men love feels impelled to embrace not only the world of the living but also the world of the dead, the underworld and the world of the as yet unborn—that is, the whole race of Adam. And if love rejoices and is glad at the salvation of a brother, she also weeps and prays over a brother who perishes.

I asked the Staretz how anyone could love all men, and

where it was possible to find the love that made a man one with all men.

He answered:

'To be one with all, as the Lord said, "that all may be one," there is no need for us to cudgel our brains: we all have one and the same nature, and so it should be natural for us to love all men; but it is the Holy Spirit who gives the strength to love.'

The power of love is vast and pregnant with success but it does not override. There is a domain in human life where a limit is set even to love—where love is not supreme. This domain is freedom.

Man's freedom is positive, real. It concedes no determinism in his destiny, so that neither the sacrifice of Christ Himself nor the sacrifices of all those who have trodden in His footsteps lead necessarily to victory. There may be some—whether many or few, we do not know—who will meet even this perfect love, this perfect sacrifice, with a rejection, even on the eternal plane, and declare, 'I want no part in it'. (It was their recognition of this abyss of freedom which prompted the Fathers of the Church to repudiate the determinist theories of the Origenists. Belief in Apocatastasis, understood as universal salvation predestined in the divine purpose, would certainly rule out the sort of prayer that we see in the Staretz.)

What was made known to the Staretz in his vision of Christ outweighed all doubt and hesitation. He *knew* that it was the Almighty God who had appeared to him. He was sure that the humility of Christ which he had come to know, and the love which filled him to the limits of his strength, were the action of God the Holy Spirit. He knew in the Holy Spirit that God is boundless love and mercy, yet knowledge of this truth did not lead him to conclude that 'anyway, we shall all be saved'.

The Staretz was unlettered but no one surpassed him in craving for true knowledge. The path he took was, however, quite unlike that of speculative philosophers. Knowing this, I followed with the deepest interest the way in which the most heterogeneous theological problems were distilled in the alembic of his mind, to emerge in his consciousness as solutions. He could not develop a question dialectically and express it in a system of rational concepts—he was afraid of 'erring in intellectual argument'; but the propositions he pronounced bore the imprint of exceptional profundity. One found oneself wondering whence came his wisdom.

The Staretz' whole existence testified to the fact that knowledge of the highest spiritual truths is to be found in the keeping of the Gospel commandments and not in surface schooling. He lived by God, and his thoughts on the profoundest of religious problems are clearly the consequence of ascetic efforts in prayer and divine visitations of grace.

Christianity is not a philosophy, not a doctrine, but *life*; and all the Staretz' conversations and writings are witness to this life.

Love for Enemies

Just as every rationalistic system has its logical sequence, its dialectics, so the spiritual world has—if we are to apply the conventional terms—its structure and its dialectics. But the argument of spiritual experience is peculiar to itself and does not follow the ordinary process of reasoning. Rationalists may, therefore, find it strange that the Staretz should regard the presence of love for enemies as the criterion of true faith, of true communion with God, and a sign of the real action of grace. Let me try to explain.

To man has been given the hope of receiving in the world to come the gift of divine likeness and full beatitude. The best he can have in this world, however, is a pledge of this future state. Within the confines of his earthly experience it is given to him to be able during prayer to dwell in God while remembering the world. But when he arrives at a more complete abiding in God the 'world is forgotten', just as a man who 'cleaves to the earth' with his whole self forgets God.

But how is it possible to speak of love for enemies as the criterion of true communion with the Divine, if in his more complete abiding in God a man forgets the world? If he forgets the world he thinks of neither friend nor foe.

God Who in His substance is supra-terrestrial, trans-
cendent, is none the less immanent in the world by reason of
His action upon it. And this immanence of activity in no way
violates the fulness and perfection of God's transcendence.
But man here on earth, clothed in flesh, possesses no such perfection, and so when he abides wholly—with all his mind and
heart—in God, he is no longer aware of the world. This must
not, however, lead us to conclude that fulness of life in God is
not connected with love for enemies. The Staretz always
asserted that the two were most closely bound together.

In his vision of the Lord he was given a degree of knowledge
that leaves no room for doubt, and he emphatically declared
that the man who loves God through the Holy Spirit must
necessarily love the whole of God's creation, too, and man first
and foremost. This love he saw as the gift of the Holy Spirit:
he looked upon it as power from on High. And inversely, he
also experienced that complete absorption in God which
springs from a blessed love for one's fellow men.

When he spoke of 'enemies' the Staretz was merely using
current language. His own attitude was different. He would say
that for Christ there are no enemies—there are those who
accept 'the words of eternal life', there are those who reject and
even crucify; but for the Creator of every living thing there can
be no enemy. So it should be for the Christian, too, who 'in
pity for all must strive for the salvation of all'.

Wherein, then, lies the force of the commandment, *Love
your enemies*? Why did the Lord say that those who keep His
commandments would know from very experience *whence* was
the doctrine? How did the Staretz interpret this?

God is love, in superabundance embracing all creatures. By
allowing man actually to know this love the Holy Spirit
reveals to him the path to fulness of being. To say 'enemy'
implies rejection. By such rejection a man falls from the
plenitude of God. Those who have attained the Kingdom of
Heaven and abide in God in the Holy Spirit behold every
abyss of hell, for there is no domain in all existence where God
could not be. 'The whole paradise of Saints lives by the Holy
Spirit, and from the Holy Spirit nothing in creation is hid,'

writes the Staretz. 'God is love and in the Saints the Holy Spirit is love. Dwelling in the Holy Spirit, the Saints behold hell and embrace it, too, in their love.'

Because a man cannot simultaneously dwell wholly in God and wholly in the world it is possible to judge whether a given state of contemplation was a reality or an illusion only after the soul has returned to consciousness of the world; for then, as the Staretz pointed out, if there were no love for enemies and so for all creatures, it would be a true indication that the supposed contemplation had not been a real communion with God.

'Ecstasy' in contemplation can come to a man before he is aware of it, and he can fail to understand what has befallen him, even if it come not from God. And if the fruit of his contemplation after his 'return' is a proud indifference to the fate of the world and the destinies of man, it was certainly fallacious. Thus, the truth or fraudulency of contemplation is known by its fruits.

Both Christ's commandments—of love towards God and love towards our neighbour—make up a single way of life. Therefore, if a man believes that he lives in and loves God but he hates his brother, he is deluded. In this manner the second commandment affords us the possibility of examining how far we are living in the true God.

On the Word of God and the Potentiality of Created Man

Every human thought, every human word is a form of energy. Immeasurably more is this true of the word of God.

When we hear the Gospel words of Christ, those fragrant gentle sayings—'Blessed are the pure in heart: for they shall see God'; or 'This is my commandment, That ye love one another'; or 'Learn of me; for I am meek and lowly in heart'—we must not forget that these words of Christ are that infinite power which called from the darkness of non-being into the light of life all that is, all the worlds without end, all creatures reasoning and unreasoning.

Just as the Word co-eternal with the Father became visible

and tangible to man through the Incarnation, so, too, was the word-idea of Christ clothed in the humble form of human language which can even be recorded in writing. Nevertheless, this word in its metaphysical roots is the energy of Almighty God which, as was said of God Himself, is the 'consuming fire', to be approached by mortals 'with reverence and godly fear'.

Christ's word is the most mysterious of words, beyond the reach of even the greatest intellects, yet withal so simple and lucid that it is easy for little children to grasp.

Christ's word is, on the one hand, so close to us, so deeply kin to the human heart; on the other, so utterly transcending the capacity of the created mind—Divine, inscrutable and, as St Paul says, 'not of man and not after man'. Its authority is absolute, since it is the word of the sole Master of the universe. 'Heaven and earth shall pass away: but my words shall not pass away,' said Christ.

The word of Christ, accepted with deep faith, leads man to eternal life along a path where he will encounter much that is extraordinary and unfamiliar to those who do not tread in Christ's footsteps. On this lofty highroad all that man can have of experience and knowledge in his life will be disclosed to him. The light of Christ's word reaches to the very bottom of the dark abyss, exposing the nature of many seeming truths which fascinate humanity. The word of Christ is fire that tries 'every man's work'—that tries all that exists—for as St Paul testifies: 'Neither is there any creature that is not manifest in his sight'.

The word of Christ is spirit and life eternal, the fulness of love and joy of the heavenly hosts. The word of Christ is un-created divine light—addressed not to superficial logical reason but to the deep heart of man, and he who opens wide his whole heart in order to receive this divine light, and be made one with it, becomes in the likeness of God.

Thus assimilated, the word of Christ makes a god of man.

The experience of the great ascetics shows that they were

concerned with the entire range of life's problems—indeed, with the whole field of dogmatic inquiry—but in special circumstances that had nothing to do with academic investigation. The human spirit is led by the Spirit of Christ to existential knowledge of God.

When I say that the Christian ascetic is made free of man's greatest potentialities; when I speak of the fulness of Christian—that is, of pan-human—experience, I do not mean experience of the various professions or branches of scientific knowledge, or social and economic conditions, *et caetera,* but of man's potential experience of the fall, and of repentance and resurrection in Christ.

Knowledge of the first kind belongs to 'things temporal', whereas the experience of redemption and resurrection in Christ is an experience of 'things eternal'. The former is characterised by diffusion and endless diversity; the latter makes manifest man's likeness to God and the ontological oneness of the human race. Where the first experience exists it can add nothing to the second, and can take nothing from it when it does not. The spirit of man is such that the limitations he suffers in the outside world cannot prevent a full experience on the spiritual plane. In the last extreme, experience in Christ does not depend on external conditions. The commandments of Christ have an absolute character, and there are and can be no physical circumstances in which it would be totally impossible to obey.

But is it not claiming too much to say that Christian experience plumbs the depths of pan-human life? Does not this experience relate to just one among the many aspects of cosmic being, which is composed of divers realities, each the subject of one or another form of knowledge like science, art, philosophy, mysticism, and so forth?

In speaking of plumbing the depths of human potentiality I take as my starting point the argument that every reasoning creature moves between two poles: one—love of God to the point of hatred of self; the other—love of self to the point of hatred of God. Every reasoning creature is thus conditioned. Whatever we do is the product of our spiritual self-determination precisely in this polarised movement, whether it is a conscious process or whether it springs from the irrational depths of our spirit.

God calls all men without exception. But not all respond to the call of His love. Those who do, with their whole being, meet with manifold trials, often extraordinarily severe. Those who love God suffer torments not to be endured by the man of little faith who inevitably becomes mentally disturbed. But faith and love of Christ beget great courage, which saves people from falling ill when they encounter evil spirits. They know the suffering yet, in spite of their experience, they not only remain normally sane—that is, they do not lose their self-possession, their mental and moral control—but their faculties attain an incomparably greater depth and refinement than is to be found in the average man.

God is invisible, and the spiritual paths to Him are unseen. Who can describe in words this mysterious life? The protests of reason will detach the follower of Christ from love of God—reason being incapable of containing the word of Christ which appears to be utter folly. Sometimes desire for the delights of this life will separate the ascetic from the love of God, sometimes fear of pain and death. Now he will be tempted by the sublimity and light of other experiences and achievements; or by the magnitude of other possessions or possibilities. At times he will be led astray by visions of angels and other heavenly bodies, at times by the violence of dark and terrifying forces.

Contact with the Staretz convinced me that all human paths are known to the Christian ascetic, while his own path remains hidden from alien eyes. 'But he that is spiritual judgeth all things, yet he himself is judged of no man. For who hath known the mind of the Lord, that he may instruct him? But we have the mind of Christ.'

6

Pure Prayer and Mental Stillness

THE Staretz loved the long church Offices, so rich in spiritual content. Yet with all his affection for the majesty, beauty and music of divine service he would declare that the offices, though instituted by the grace of the Holy Spirit, are but an imperfect form of prayer, given to the faithful as being adapted to the strength of, and beneficial for, all men.

'The Lord gave us church offices with singing because we are helpless children: we do not yet know how to pray aright, whereas singing is good for all men when they sing in humility. But it is a better thing for our hearts to become the church of the Lord and our minds His altar.'

And again:

'The Lord is glorified in holy temples, while monks and anchorites praise God in their hearts. The heart of the anchorite is a temple and his mind an altar, for the Lord loves to dwell in the heart and mind of man.'

And he would say, too, that when unceasing prayer becomes established in the depths of the heart all the world is transformed into a temple of God.

The whole of Blessed Staretz Silouan's life was prayer. He prayed unceasingly, in the course of the day changing the mode of his prayer to accord with the circumstances of the daily round. He had, too, the greater gift of mental prayer, to which he chiefly devoted the night hours in the complete silence and darkness propitious to this form of prayer, which consists in guarding the heart from every alien thought, through the exercise of inner recollectedness, so that no foreign influence should disturb communion with God. This discipline may be termed variously sacred silence (hesychia), inner quiet or mental stillness. We have inherited it through the living and written tradition of the holy Fathers: it has come down to us from the first centuries of Christian history. To describe the path followed by the Staretz in his spiritual life is therefore to describe the course of Orthodox monasticism in general.

The Staretz said: 'If thou art a divine, thou prayest purely. If thou prayest purely, then thou art a divine.'

A monk leading the ascetic life is not a theologian in the academic sense; but he is a theologian in the sense that pure prayer prepares him for divine contemplation.

The ascent to pure prayer begins with the struggle with the passions. As the mind becomes cleansed of passion it grows stronger in the fight against intrusive thoughts, and more steadfast in prayer and meditation; while the heart, in liberating itself from the darkening effects of passion, begins to see spiritual things more clearly and more purely, and finally acquires an intuitive certitude about them.

The monk prefers this to scientific theology because while it is possible through abstract, philosophic contemplation to come to realise that our human conceptions are not applicable to God, and thus to arrive at the state where the mind starts to be 'silent', this silence of the mind is in nowise always true contemplation of God, though it approaches the borders of true contemplation.

Unless the heart be cleansed it is impossible to attain real contemplation. Only a heart purified of passion is capable of that peculiar awe and wonder before God which stills the mind into joyful silence.

The theologian-thinker aims at contemplation by one means, the monk-ascetic by another. The main object of the monk is to achieve the stillness of prayer in the heart, with the mind, free from reflections, keeping quiet watch like a sentry to make sure that nothing enters into the heart from without. Where this state of sacred silence exists, heart and mind feed on the Name of Christ and His commandments. They live as one, controlling all happenings within, not by logical investigation but intuitively, by a specific spiritual sense.

So soon as the mind unites with the heart it can see every movement in the sphere of the subconscious. (I borrow this term from contemporary scientific psychology although it does not exactly correspond with the theory of Orthodox asceticism concerning anthropology.) While the mind dwells in the heart it perceives the images and thoughts around it proceeding from the sphere of cosmic being which attempt to seize heart and mind. The energy of this or that spirit makes itself manifest in the form of thought-suggestion roused by this or that image. The attack of intrusive thoughts is fierce. To weaken their onset the monk is constrained the livelong day not to admit a single passionate consideration, not to allow himself a predilection of any kind. His constant aim is to reduce the number of outside impressions to its very minimum. Otherwise, at the time of inner mental prayer, all the impressions of the day will crowd unrestrained into his heart, causing the greatest disturbance.

The mind deeply wrapped in prayer senses at times the approach of some spirit from without; but if prayerful attention is preserved uninterrupted the alien spirit goes away unadmitted, and when the ascetic has finished praying he even cannot say what kind of influence sought entry, for what reason or with what proposal.

When prayer deepens, luminous visions sometimes approach the mind and try to distract it. If the ascetic pays no heed they begin saying to him: 'We offer you wisdom and understanding, and if you do not let us in immediately you may never see us again.' But the experienced mind does not pay the slightest heed to such phenomena, with the result that they go away not only unadmitted but even unrecognised, while the mind may not even know for certain whether what approached was an evil spirit or a good angel. But it knows by experience that prayer is lost, and hard indeed to recapture, if the attention is allowed to dwell on the glittering fantasies which present themselves. Experience has proved that in the hour of prayer one must not linger even on an apparently good thought, for it is sure to bring with it other intrusive thoughts, so that, as the Staretz said, the mind will not emerge pure. And nothing can make up for the loss of pure prayer.

The end the monk-ascetic strives after is a state of

uninterrupted mental attention in the heart—a state in which prayer becomes constant, imbued with a clear, robust feeling of God present and active, and the mind from much weeping becomes strong enough to push back every attack by passionate intrusive thoughts.

The Staretz believed that the essence of spiritual quiet lay not in living the life of a hermit or retiring to the desert but in a constant dwelling in God. He said that both the recluse's way of life and the way of the desert solitary were simply means, never ends in themselves. They might help by diminishing external impressions and influences and keeping man aloof from life's sound and fury, thus favouring pure prayer, but only if such retirement from the world conforms to the will of God and is not merely man's personal choice. A hermit's life, or any other kind of ascetic striving, will be sterile if it is self-willed, because the essential is not that we should arbitrarily perform ascetic feats but that we should be obedient to the will of God.

The Staretz thought that no one mode of ascetic endeavour was *per se* the highest form of spiritual life. Prayer in a desert, a life of seclusion, the assumption of folly for Christ's sake, the ministry or learned work in the field of theology—any one of these would be the highest way for a given person if it corresponded to God's will for him. Even so, when considering this or that kind of spiritual effort, this or that place or manner in which to serve God, the quest for pure prayer remains imperative and the ultimate aim.

Man's Personal Relationship to a Personal God

The Lord said to Pontius Pilate: 'For this cause came I into the world, that I should bear witness unto the truth.'

'What is truth?' queried Pilate sceptically, and, convinced that there was no answer to that question, he did not stay for one, even from Christ, but went out again to the Jews.

Pilate was right. To the question '*What* is truth?' there is no answer if we mean the ultimate truth, the foundation of the world's whole existence. But if Pilate had had in mind the

Original Truth or the Truth of Truths, and had phrased his question as it should have been phrased—if he had asked '*Who* is truth?'—he would have received the answer, 'I am the truth,' which is what the Lord, in the foreknowledge of Pilate's question, had said to His beloved disciples a few hours before at the Last Supper, and through them to the world at large.

Science and philosophy ask themselves: *What* is truth? while genuine Christian religious consciousness is always directed towards the truth that is *Who*.

Scientists and philosophers often look upon Christians as ill-founded dreamers, while considering that they themselves stand on sure ground, which is why they call themselves positivists. Strangely, they do not understand the full negative extent of their '*What*'. They do not understand that real truth, absolute Truth can only be 'Who', and never 'What', because Truth is no abstract formula or idea but Life itself.

What, indeed, could be more abstract or more negative than truth in the form of 'what'? This great paradox is seen all through the history of mankind since Adam's fall. Bewitched by its own powers of reasoning, humanity lives in a sort of vertigo, so that not only do 'positive' science and philosophy set themselves, like Pilate, the question *What* is truth? but even in the religious life of mankind the same radical misconception is to be observed: the continual search for truth as *what*. Reason supposes that once this sought-after truth is found man will become master of magic powers and free arbiter of existence.

The truth that is *Who* cannot be obtained through the exertions of the human reason. God as Who is only made known through a communion in being, that is, through the Holy Spirit. The Staretz stressed this point constantly.

The Lord Himself declared:

'If a man love me, he will keep my words: and my Father will love him, and we will come unto him, and make our abode with him ... The Comforter, which is the Holy Ghost, whom the Father will send in my name, he shall teach you all things.'

Orthodox ascetic experience rejects abstract contemplation and considers that neither the man who in his meditations on

God dwells on abstract contemplation of Goodness, Beauty, Eternity, Love and so on, nor the one who merely strips his mind of all empirical images and conceptions, has found the true path. True contemplation is given by God through the advent of God into the soul. Then the soul contemplates God and sees that He loves, that He is good, magnificent, eternal; she beholds His transcendence and ineffability.

Genuine spiritual life, which is utterly concrete and positive, excludes the imagination. There is no other way for man to seek intercourse with the Divine than by personal prayer to a Personal God.

The appearance of Christ to Staretz Silouan was a *personal* meeting which afterwards made his way of addressing God deeply personal. When he prayed he talked face to Face with God. This feeling of meeting a Personal God cleanses prayer from imagination and abstract speculations, and centres it in a certain invisible, inner, living communion. Prayer ceases to be 'invocation into space'—the movement is inward and the mind becomes all attention, concentrated to listen. When the Staretz invoked the name of God—Father, Lord or any of the other appellations he used—he was in that state about which 'it is not lawful for a man' to speak; but whoever has experienced the presence of the living God will understand.

Prayer 'face to Face' is the vital prelude to man's discovery in himself of the 'image of God', so let us consider this side of our life in God.

The final stage of Revelation is the revelation of a Personal God—a *Hypostatic* God. (I prefer the Greek word ὑπόστασις, to avoid the technicalities of the terms *individual* or *personal*.) The Hypostatic God can only be known through revelation—by God appearing to man in an act of direct contact, 'Face to face'. It is indispensable that God should first manifest Himself to us.

When God as Hypostasis reveals Himself to man in this direct contact, even though it is still 'as in a glass', man will become aware of his own hypostasy, in which the 'likeness of

God' is reflected first and foremost. Man, 'being flesh and living in the world' experiences primarily his own limited individuality, and this new expanded consciousness is like a birth from on High. 'Except a man be born again, he cannot see the kingdom of God.' After such a birth prayer assumes a different character, outstripping the bounds of time and matter, and man feels caught up into the eternity of God.

Revelation of the Hypostatical God leads to the realisation that hypostasis is the form of Absolute Being; that this dimension—hypostasis—is not limitative but He Who lives indeed: the I AM (cf. Exodus 3. 14 and John 8. 58). Outside this dimension nothing exists nor can exist. There is no 'essence' beyond the Hypostasis in Divine Being. And so the Christian's prayer is addressed to the Hypostatic God, 'face to Face': it is not a search for or a turning to a Supra-Personal Essence.

This knowledge makes plain, therefore, that we are *created* hypostases, endowed with freedom for a self-determination which can be either positive in relation to the Prototype, or negative.

A free, non-pre-determined hypostasis can only be created as pure potentiality, intended to be actualised subsequently. So, then, we are not yet entirely hypostases: we are going through the more or less lengthy process of becoming—of converting an 'atomised' into a hypostatic form of being. The concept of person-hypostasis must not be confused with the concept of the individual—(in Greek ἄτομον, the result of the fall of man). They are actually two poles of the human being. One expresses the last degree of division, the other indicates the 'image of God' in which Adam was made, in whose entrails all mankind was potentially enclosed. This is the pattern manifested to us by the Word made flesh. In our apprehension of God, therefore, we do not transfer our experience of the limitation of the individual to Divine Being, in order afterwards to deny in Him the hypostatic character and, consequently, cast about for a Supra-Personal Absolute. The impulse of our spirit is towards prayer face to Face—prayer, that is, of the created hypostasis to the

Hypostasis of God. It is essential that the hypostatic principle be unfolded in us. What are the ways and means to this end?

Called forth from non-being, we are all of us bound by the fetters of relative time and relative space. The spirit of man, the image of the absolute God, is cramped within the framework of this material world. Man feels trapped, like a condemned prisoner. His suffering approaches despair, from which springs prayer of a singular tension, prayer 'against hope believing in hope'. It may be that all of us, people of our time, need this experience of despair during the course of our birth unto eternity.

Arriving in the world the child learns first from his mother and father, then from friends and teachers. Grown to man's estate, he seizes eagerly on knowledge of every kind until finally he may become convinced that 'scientific' knowledge not only fails to carry him beyond the relative dimensions of time and space but, worse, constricts his consciousness within the determinist aspect of existence.

Our spirit's refusal to accept the absurdity of death as a return into nothingness engenders fervent prayer and a diligent search in Holy Writ for knowledge of the Eternal. No school, however—and that includes theological schools—no books, even sacred books, can, without the utmost ascetic effort of our whole being in pure prayer, make us feel that God has heard and accepted us into His eternity.

This prayer born of 'despair' is without doubt a gift from on High. It sets us on the borderline between time and eternity. Time is, as it were, forgotten, somewhere at the back of us, and the gaze of our spirit fastens on eternity, still out of reach, still not in our possession. This transposition of the spirit in prayer to the ultimate boundaries of time explains much in the Scriptures that has hitherto seemed paradoxical—as, for instance, 'One day is with the Lord as a thousand years, and a thousand years as one day'; 'Ye were ... redeemed ... by the precious blood of Christ, as of a lamb without blemish and without spot: Who verily was foreordained before the foundation of the world, but was manifest in these last times': 'Now all these things ... are written for our admonition, upon whom the ends of the world are come'; 'He hath chosen us ... before the foundation of the world'; and, lastly, 'I write unto you ... because ye have known him that is from the beginning'.

What do the words 'these last times' or 'the end of the world' mean? What are we to understand in the Liturgy of St John Chrysostom by 'Thou hadst bestowed upon us Thy kingdom to come'; or 'We have seen the figure of Thy Resurrection, we have been filled with Thine immortal life' in St Basil the Great's Liturgy?

Because of their immediate contact with the Divine Hypostasis of the Logos, the Apostles, while still here on earth, in spirit sojourned also in Eternity. For them, as for everyone else experiencing a similar state, Time-Aeon draws to an end. (Their perception of time differed from that of Newton and Einstein or philosophers and gnostics of varying moulds.) For them time becomes a sort of 'space' admitting of change of position, 'where' a first meeting with the Creator is possible. We read that it was given to some to see 'the kingdom of God come with power' before they 'tasted of death'. Such people have a particular perception of the world.

The ways of the Lord are in this wise: To begin with, He seeks us, reveals His 'Face' to us, draws us into His eternity. Then he may return us to the framework of time. There would seem to be no sense in this return other than to entrust us to manifest in our life the knowledge given to us of the I AM, and bear witness to His love for us. We ourselves, however, feel our return as an 'absence from the Lord', as a withdrawal of grace, and we weary under the burden of the mortal body. The craving to restore the lost fulness of union with God urges one to spiritual effort, which—a human act, now—becomes an ascetic science, an art, a culture. In our age this culture is largely abandoned or forgotten.

Orthodox ascetic culture has many aspects. One of these is monastic or, rather, Christian obedience. Let me at this point try to supplement what has been said earlier about obedience, and endeavour to express some of the essential tenets concerning the meaning and results of this ascetic striving.

Obedience, like every great culture, can be interpreted on various levels, dependent on the individual's spiritual age. At the beginning obedience may be little more than a passive inclination of the will to that of the spiritual father, springing from trust in him and a desire for deeper knowledge of the divine will. In a more perfected form obedience becomes a positive activity of the spirit straining to follow the commandments of Christ Who loved mankind with an immeasurable love.

Whoever would progress in the practice of obedience must turn his attention and will towards apprehending his brother's will, and then in an act of spiritual love implementing it. Such an act of obedience broadens the heart, enriches the mind and brings new life to the soul. In its subsequent development the spiritual feat of obedience leads to a more sensitive response to every other human being and to an awareness of God's image in him, thus providing an indication of the state of development of one's own 'humanity'. St John the Divine writes: 'If a man say, I love God, and hateth his brother, he is a liar: for he that loveth not his brother whom he hath seen, how can he love God whom he hath not seen? And this commandment have we from him, That he who loveth God love his brother also.' Likewise, 'If ye love me, keep my commandments.' The sequence is similar in the field of obedience. He who loves his brother will naturally want to accomplish his will and incline to him; and if we do not incline to our brother and perform our obedience to him in ways which are always more or less secondary, how can we incline before God and be obedient to His holy and eternal Will? How fulfil the commandment to love our neighbour as ourself, or to love enemies? The spiritual feat of obedience is vital, therefore, not only in relation to God but to our brother, too, when the latter would have something of us that is not impossible or against the spirit of God's commandments.

The painful effort of obedience to our brother develops in us the ability to penetrate more deeply into the Divine Will, and this likens man to the Only-Begotten Son of the Father, and makes him a bearer in spirit of all mankind. In other words, he becomes universal with a universality akin to that of Christ Himself.

Without this truly Christian culture of obedience man inevitably remains imprisoned in a closed circle, ever blind to the divine purpose. However learned one may be, without the obedience of the Gospels the door into one's inner world remains tightly shut, and Christ's love cannot penetrate within.

The mentally ill can grasp neither another person's idea nor his will. Thus the lack of obedience in one's disposition is the surest sign of spiritual sickness which confines one in the clutches of selfish individuality (the opposite principle to hypostasy) and to a greater or lesser degree makes one deaf to divine revelation as given to us on the plane of History by the hypostatic incarnation of the Logos. It can be said that true theology, understood as a state of being in communion with God, is unattainable outside the culture of Christian obedience.

Christian obedience is a noble culture, and we need either the wisdom of a 'naïve' faith or the prolonged effort of prayer if our eyes are to be opened to its majesty and holiness.

Progressing in the art of obedience, one becomes not only more sensitive and alert to other people's ideas and will, and more understanding of their needs, but at the same time learns to experience one's own condition, not within the narrow framework of one's individuality but as a kind of revelation of what is happening in the world at large. Every form of pain and suffering, physical or mental, every success or defeat, is lived, not only within the self, 'selfishly', but is transferred in spirit to other people, for at any given moment there are certainly millions in a state similar to ours. The natural sequence to this realisation is prayer for the whole world. When we pray for the living, we share their joy in love, their grief at loss, or the terrible darkness of their despair. Having experienced pain, we pray for all who are sick and suffering: we lean in thought over the beds of those who, lonely and distressed, lie helplessly facing death. To think of the dead plunges our spirit into the depths of past centuries, or else our mind fixes on the invisible but dread path along which hundreds of thousands of souls pass every day, having left their bodies often after excruciating agony. In this fashion those who practise obedience develop Christian compassion for the torment of all humanity, and their prayers take on a cosmic dimension embracing the whole Adam—in other words, their prayer becomes *hypostatic,* after the manner of Christ's prayer at Gethsemane. This sort of prayer makes man aware of his unity with all mankind, and to love his neighbour—his fellow man—evolves into a natural impulse. Such prayer effectively furthers the salvation of the world, and every Christian must sooner or later come to prayer for the whole world. Especially is this true of priests celebrating the Divine Liturgy.

The principle of 'personalist' obedience is closely tied to the theology of the Person-Hypostasis which, in its turn, proceeds from the right understanding of revelation concerning the Holy Trinity, each Hypostasis of Which possesses the absolute fulness of Divine Being. To lose sight of this theology leads to a search, conscious or unconscious, for some trans-personal principle and a consequent preference for the general rather than the individual. Obedience is then required not to another person but to the law, the rule, the function, the institution, *et caetera.* In this sort of impersonal approach to the structure of human life the true meaning of Christian obedience as expressed in the commandments of Christ is lost, to be replaced by human 'discipline'. (Of course discipline is inevitable in the present state of society, if life in common is to be co-ordinated, but it must not be overdone.)

Failure to appreciate the theological vision of the person, and so to neglect the effort towards evangelical obedience, cannot be compensated by any apparent success of the institution or harmonious structure of the depersonalised whole.

The noblest mission of the Church of Christ lies not in the acquisition of material well-being or political power—'For what is a man advantaged, if he gain the whole world, and lose himself, or be cast away?'—but in the raising of her faithful sons 'unto the measure of the stature of the fulness of Christ'.

Tokens of Grace and Beguilement

I once asked the Staretz whether there was any certain sign to enable one to distinguish the true spiritual path from those phantom tracks which lie on either side of it. This is what he replied:

'Sometimes the Holy Spirit draws a man so wholly to Himself that he forgets all created things and gives himself entirely to contemplation of God. But when the soul remembers the world again, filled with love of God she feels compassion for all and prays for the whole world. In thus praying, the soul may again forget the world and repose in the One God, only to return once more to her prayer for all mankind.

'The Holy Spirit teaches us to love God and our neighbour; but the spirit that beguiles is a proud spirit sparing neither man nor the rest of creation because it has created nothing. Its path is strewn with destruction. The spirit of beguilement cannot bestow true sweetness but merely the restless sweetness of vainglory. There is neither humility nor peace nor love in it: only a cold indifferent pride.

'The Holy Spirit teaches the love of God, and the soul yearns for God and with tears seeks Him day and night; but the enemy brings anguish, heavy and overcast, which destroys the soul.

'By these tokens can the grace of God be distinguished from the beguilement of the enemy.'

Christ's Commandment—to Love God with all the Mind, and with all the Heart—as the Foundation of Mental Stillness

Certain of the holy Fathers draw a distinction between the

two kinds of spiritual life, active and contemplative, calling the first the way of the commandments.

Staretz Silouan thought somewhat differently. He, too, divided life into active and contemplative, but with the keeping of the commandments as the sole intention in each case. The first commandment, to 'love God with all thy heart, with all thy mind, with all thy soul,' was, in his view, the keystone of ascetic mental quiet. He wrote:

'The man who has come to know the love of God will say to himself: I have not kept this commandment. Though I pray day and night, and strive to practise every virtue, still I have failed in the commandment of love towards God. Only at rare moments do I arrive at God's commandment, though my soul longs at all times to abide in it. When irrelevant thoughts intrude into the mind, the mind is then concerned both with God and with them, and so the commandment to love God with *all* thy mind and *all* thy heart is not fulfilled. But when the mind is entirely wrapped in God, to the exclusion of every other thought—that is to fulfil the first commandment, though again not completely.'

God is absolutely free. No incantation or attempt at compulsion can constrain Him. Inner quiet attended by stubborn self-renouncement is one of the hardest endeavours of the spiritual life. Spontaneous acceptance—the better to observe God's commandments—of the suffering entailed attracts God's grace but only when the striving is done in a spirit of humility. That is why the Staretz in his struggle for humility seized on the fiery weapon given him by the Lord:

'Keep thy mind in hell, and despair not.'

Intellectually he was 'unlearned and ignorant' but he repeatedly achieved true contemplation, and so, well-founded, could say: 'There are many on earth who believe but very few among them *know* God.'

Knowledge he understood not as cognitive theological formation but as lively experience of union, of communion in the Divine Light.

For him, knowing meant a *sharing of being*.

Recollection of Death and Experience of Eternity

Experience of eternity begins with recollection of death, which in the works of the Fathers does not refer to man's normal awareness of his mortality, or to the simple consciousness that one day we shall die. It is a particular spiritual feeling which derives from a sense of the shortness of our earthly existence. Now waning, now waxing, this 'remembrance of death' is at times transformed into a profound sensation of the corruptible and transitory nature of all earthly matter, which modifies man's attitude to everything in the world: whatever is not eternal becomes of little value, and the absurdity of acquiring earthly possessions apparent. The mind's attention is turned from the surrounding external world, to be focused within, where the soul is faced by incomprehensible unending darkness. This reduces the soul to terror which in turn gives birth to intense prayer, prayer that can be restrained neither by night nor by day. Time stands still, not at first because the soul has beheld the light of eternal life but, on the contrary, because she is engulfed by a feeling of eternal death. At last, by degrees, the soul is led through divine action into the domain of light without beginning. And this is no philosophic 'transcendentalism' but a genuine manifestation of life, requiring no logical proofs. It is indefinable, unprovable, inexplicable knowledge and, being life itself, for all its impossibility of definition, incomparably more powerful and inwardly convincing than the most impeccable abstract dialectic.

Time and eternity, as understood by the ascetic, are two different modes of being. Time is the mode of the creature, incomprehensibly created by God out of nothing, and for ever quickening and evolving. Eternity is the mode of Divine Being to which our conceptions of extension and succession do not apply. Eternity is a unique act of Divine Being, an act of incomprehensible fulness, which, being supra-terrestrial, embraces the whole expanse of the created world. Only the One God is eternal in substance. Eternity is not an abstraction, something existing separately, but is God Himself in His own

Being. When it is God's good pleasure to give man grace and make him a sharer in Divine Life, man becomes not only immortal in the sense of having his life endlessly prolonged—which would be a vicious infinity—but beginningless, too, for the sphere of Divine Life into which he is lifted has neither beginning nor end. By 'beginningless' I do not mean to imply a pre-existence of the soul or a transmutation of our created nature into *unoriginate* Divine Nature: I mean a sharing in God's unoriginate life consequent on the deification of the creature by an act of grace.

Man discovers his real self when mind and heart, turned towards Christ, are joined, not by his own efforts but by the action of God, in mystic union. He then, as an immortal person, his mind made in God's image, his spirit god-like, sightlessly beholds the Lord. Yet so long as he is tied to the flesh his knowledge will not attain perfection. He will not be able to fathom what his eternal existence will be like once he has been delivered of the grossness of the earthly body and, unburdened, has entered 'into that within the veil', should God see fit to receive his soul. But he will not wonder about eternal life in moments of vision when the soul is entirely in the eternal God and does not know whether she is in the body or outside it, but only when the soul sees the world again and once more feels herself fettered by her corporeal bonds.

Man does not possess eternal life in himself—that is, within the confines of his created being. He becomes eternal by a gift of grace when he communicates in Divine Life. In so far as we are in God, we are eternal. (*In so far* is meant here not in a quantitative sense but applies to the nature of the gifts granted by God.)

The soul in a state of vision has no questions to ask. She does not bring about by her own will the indescribable act which introduces her into the divine world, because she cannot desire what she has never known. Still, this act does not take place without her participation, in that at some preliminary moment of her own free will she has ardently aspired towards God in the keeping of His commandments. The prelude to vision is suffering and the repentance which comes from the deep heart, those scalding tears which burn up in man the pride of flesh and spirit.

Man while he is in the flesh cannot attain perfect knowledge but God does give him an actual, indubitable, existential experience of the Eternal Kingdom. He may know 'in part', as the Staretz said, but his knowledge is sure.

Concerning Prayer for the World

The Blessed Staretz wrote: 'A monk is a man who prays for the whole world.' Prayer for the whole world often means not caring for individual people. It may be objected that this is a denial of the concrete in favour of the abstract, which is not true, since Adam's breed is no abstraction but the most actual plenitude of human being.

'Perhaps,' continues the Staretz, 'you will say that nowadays there are no monks who would pray for the whole world; but I tell you that when we have no more men of prayer the world will come to an end and great disaster will befall—as, indeed, is happening already.'

There are people who, strangely, do not understand the immense power of prayer. They look on the religious life in general and prayer in particular as a series of subjective psychological experiences which lose all validity as soon as they terminate in the soul. From long contact with the Staretz and his writings I realised that he regarded spiritual states as evidence of divine action in man, and therefore as being of ontological order. He felt prayer for enemies and for the world at large as an especial gift of the Holy Spirit; and that so long as there were vessels for this grace in the world, the world would continue to exist but without them no human science, no culture could avert the final catastrophe.

Saints live on the love of Christ, the Divine Strength which created and upholds the world, and it is for this reason that their prayers are so powerful. Every saint is a phenomenon of a cosmic order, the importance of which goes far beyond the bounds of history into the realm of eternity. The saints are the salt of the earth. They are the fruit for the sake of which the world is preserved. But when the earth ceases to bring forth saints, it will be bereft of the strength that keeps it from calamity.

Experience daily shows that even people who in their hearts accept Christ's commandment to love enemies do not fulfil it in practice. Why? First of all because to love enemies, suffering and praying for them, is impossible without the action of the Holy Spirit. It exceeds our natural powers. But if we were to seek this blessed help from God, we would receive it, as the Staretz used to say.

Unfortunately, the reverse happens—not only unbelievers but those, too, who profess themselves Christian, fear to behave towards enemies according to Christ's bidding. They suppose that only the enemy would benefit—taking advantage of their 'weakness' and responding to love by crucifixion or subjection; and thus evil would triumph, the enemy being seen as the embodiment of evil.

This idea of Christianity as spineless and feeble is profoundly erroneous. The saints possess the power to dominate the masses but they choose the very opposite: they submit themselves to their fellow men and by so doing win imperishable love for themselves. Victory gained by force never lasts for long, and by its very nature brings, not glory but shame to mankind.

To love enemies makes man like unto Christ right at the heart of his being and is the beginning of his deification. This, according to the Staretz' teaching, is true faith.

'Many have studied all kinds of different confessions yet have not found the true faith. But to him who humbly prays to God for enlightenment, God will make known how greatly He loves man.'

People are afraid to cast themselves into the flame of Christ's love. They fear to be destroyed. But those who are not afraid discover that they have found eternal life, and need no evidence other than the Spirit Itself witnessing within to their salvation.

The Staretz was profoundly aware that evil can only be overcome by good. The use of force only leads to the substitution of one form of violence for another. We often talked about this, and once he said: 'The Gospel plainly states that when the Samaritans would not receive Christ, the disciples James and John wanted to bring down fire from heaven to consume them, but the Lord forbade them and said: "Ye know not what manner of spirit ye are of . . . The Son of man is not come to destroy men's lives, but to save them." And this ought to be our one thought, too—that all should be saved.'

If we look back over the history of Christianity, we are struck by the achievements of Christian culture. Huge libraries full of the noble products of the human spirit. Universities and schools, where hundreds of thousands of young people approach the shores of this great ocean with bated breath and hearts pulsing with happiness, eager to drink of the living waters of wisdom. Magnificent churches, wondrous creations of the human genius. Countless works of art—music, painting, sculpture, poetry. And much, much more. And yet the Staretz would seem to disregard it all, to take his stand on one thing alone: the humility of Christ and love for enemies. This humility of Christ and love for enemies are the sum of 'all things' ('all things that I have heard of my Father I have made known unto you'), and without them all the laws, all the prophets, all the cultures are nothing worth.

I believe that the Staretz' teaching merits the utmost attention, not superficially but with one's whole being. I have never met anyone who could prove with such conviction—or knowledge, even—that compassionate love for enemies is the only reliable criterion of truth; and this not only in the soteriological sense—that concerns the moral order of life and man's salvation—but also on the doctrinal plane in so far as it relates to intellectual conceptions of Divine Life.

The doctrinal teaching of the Church constitutes an organic, indissolubly-integral unity from which separate parts may not be arbitrarily detached. Error of any sort whatsoever will inevitably be reflected in the mode of our spiritual existence. Certain deviations in our thinking concerning God may not disastrously affect the work of salvation but there are errors and distortions which can hinder salvation.

Christ's commandment 'Love your enemies', being a projection in this world of the perfect love of the Triune God, is the final synthesis of our theology. It is the 'power from on high' and the 'life more abundant' which Christ gave to us. It is the 'baptism with the Holy Ghost' of which St John the Baptist spoke. This exhortation—love your enemies—is the fire which the Lord came to bestow on earth. It is the Uncreated Light which shone on the disciples on Mount Tabor. It is the tongues of fire in which the Holy Spirit descended on the Apostles in the upper room. It is the Kingdom of God within us 'come with power'. It is the fulness of humanity and the perfection of likeness to God (cf. Matthew 5. 44-48).

However wise and learned a man may be, however honourable his conduct, if he does not love every one of his fellow human beings he has not attained God. And, conversely, however simple and ignorant a man is, if he carries this love in his heart he dwells in God and God in him. To love enemies, to pray for them with compassion, is impossible without being in the True God, declared the Staretz. Whoever bears such love is the dwelling-place of the Holy Spirit, and by the Holy Spirit he *knows* the Father and the Son. He is the brother and friend of Christ. He is a son of God and god by grace.

7

The Struggle with the Imagination

HAVING ventured to write about the 'sacred quiet' which the Staretz so loved, I am brought to the subject of wrestling with the imagination—though I cannot hope satisfactorily to treat so difficult and complex a theme. As my principal task is to offer the reader a statement of a definite and concrete experience, I shall restrict myself to examining the views and conceptions obtaining to this day on the Holy Mountain— views and conceptions which Staretz Silouan likewise held. Contemporary psychological theories may be left on one side as having little in common with the approach of Orthodox asceticism, which proceeds from radically different cosmological and anthropological concepts.

The Staretz wrote: 'O brethren, let us forget the earth and all that is therein. The earth entices us from contemplation of the Holy Trinity, Which our minds cannot apprehend but Which the Saints in heaven behold in the Holy Spirit. We, for our part, should continue in prayer without imaginings . . . '

Imagination manifests itself in the most varied forms. First of all, the ascetic has to contend with those forms of imagination which are connected with the grosser passions. He knows that every passion has a corresponding image; and usually acquires strength in man only when the image is accepted and gains the attention of the mind. If the mind spurns the image the passion itself cannot develop, and will expire. For instance, supposing some desire of the flesh—a physiologically normal desire, maybe—comes to the ascetic, he will defend his mind from the image from without, suggested by the passion. (The word *mind* as used here denotes not reason—logical deliberation—but something which is perhaps best defined by the phrase 'inner attention'.) If the mind, understood in this sense, is preserved from passionate images complete chastity is possible throughout a whole lifetime, even when the body is strong. This is proved by the experience of centuries, and we have a further example in the Staretz. Conversely, if the mind accepts and enjoys the passionate image even a frail, diseased or exhausted body will be tyrannised.

So, too, with another passion—hatred. It, also, has an image *sui generis*. So long as the mind abstains from commerce with the image the passion cannot evolve. But if the mind unites with the image hatred will grow more and more violent, even becoming an obsession.

A second form of imagination against which the ascetic has to struggle is day-dreaming. When he gives himself over to reverie man abandons the real order of things in the world, to go and live in the domain of fantasy. Since the imagination cannot create anything out of nothing the figments engendered by it must contain elements borrowed from the actual world, just as dreams do, and therefore they are not quite unattainable: a poor man may imagine he is an emperor, a prophet, a great scientist, and history knows cases of poor men from the lowest strata of society who did rise to these high places. It is this form of the imagination which is operative in 'imaginative' prayer: by an effort of his imagination the beginner, inexperienced in spiritual combat, creates in his mind visual pictures inspired by the life of Christ, or some other sacred subject. He does not enclose his mind in his heart, for the sake of inner vigilance, but by fixing his attention on the visual images which he himself has created, but which he thinks are of divine origin, works himself into a state of emotional excitation and even morbid (pathological) ecstasy.

We see a third aspect of the power of the imagination when a man uses his faculties of memory and imagination to think out the solution to some technical problem; and when he has done so his mind will seek means for the practical realisation of his idea. This activity of the reason in association with the imagination plays a vital part in human culture and is essential for the economy of life. But the spiritual striver, whose preoccupation is to attain pure prayer, renounces every acquisition, even intellectual, lest this sort of imagining, too, hinder him from devoting his first thought and best energies to God—that is, concentrating his whole self in God.

Finally, consider the play of the imagination when the intellect attempts to penetrate the mystery of the Divine Being. The ascetic, devoting himself to active inner silence and pure prayer, resolutely combats this 'creative' impulse within himself because he sees in it a *processus* contrary to the true order of being, with man 'creating' God in his own image and likeness. The point of departure of the ascetic striving for pure prayer is the belief that God created us, not that we create God; and so he turns to Him in imageless prayer, stripped of all theological and philosophical creativeness. If grace descends upon him and it is granted to him to savour the advent of God, then this supraconceptual knowledge of God will afterwards be translated into this or that concept, not, however, of the ascetic's or prophet's own invention but received by him from above.

The ascetic seeks God his Creator through prayer, and God in His indulgence and according to His good will grants knowledge of Himself in forms accessible to man—forms which consume his passions and hallow him; but if man assumes them to be the supreme revelation he will fall into error and even the images granted from on High may become an insurmountable barrier to a more perfect knowledge of God.

God is Light inaccessible. His Being exceeds not only all corporeal but also all mental images. Therefore so long as man's mind is busied with reflection, with words, concepts and images, it has not attained the perfection of prayer.

The human mind and personality only reach the stillness of pure and perfect prayer when from love of God all created things are left behind; or, as the Staretz liked to put it, when a man utterly forgets the world and his own body so that afterwards he no longer knows whether he was in or out of the body in the hour of prayer.

Such superlatively pure prayer is a rare gift of God. It

depends not on human effort but on the power of the Lord which with infinite care and tenderness transports man into the world of Divine Light; or, as it would be better to say, Divine Light manifests itself and lovingly encompasses man's whole being so that he is no longer able either to meditate or remember anything.

Whereas the creative thought of God becomes a reality and is materialised in the world, the free movement of the created being follows the reverse direction, relinquishing things created and seeking God Himself, since in Him lie the ultimate end and meaning of man's existence. The world is not self-sufficient: it does not exist of and for itself. Its function is the final transfiguration and deification of the creature through knowledge of the Creator.

The cause of the creation of the world was God's abundant goodness. The world was not created as a means to the Incarnation of God the Word, for the Incarnation was not in the least a necessity for the Logos. The creation of the world was, therefore, in no sense a preliminary act to the Incarnation.

The gracious descent of the Logos is not a token of the intrinsic worth of the world. For understanding of its purpose and meaning we must look to the name taken by the humbly incarnate God the Word: Jesus the Saviour. 'And thou shalt call his name JESUS: for he shall save his people from their sins.'

Man's creative idea, oriented towards the world, must seek its incarnation—its realisation—if it would complete its development. But in the Divine world it is not so: the Incarnation of God the Word is not the crowning stage in a theogonic process and consequently indispensable to God Himself in order to perfect the fulness of His Being. Between the Incarnation of the Son of God and the deification of man the difference is that for God the Creator there is nothing in all that exists which could be for Him a *datum* from without, a 'fact' independent of Him. As the Creator of the form of being which we have, He was able to assume this form integrally and become consubstantial with us by His human nature. But man deified does not become consubstantial with God: he merely becomes god through grace, by a gift which he receives, though not passively—his deification cannot take place without his assent.

The dogmatic basis of mental prayer is, briefly, as follows:

Mental prayer is neither artistic creation nor scientific investigation, neither philosophic research and speculation nor abstract intellectual theology, all of which relate to the sphere of the imagination which must be overcome if one is to attain perfect prayer, true theology and a life verily pleasing to God.

Therefore, the Orthodox monk seeks the true God, the Creator, entering through mental prayer into conflict with an innumerable variety of images, some having outward forms, contours, colours and an extension in space and time, others being thought-forms—conceptions—in order to be able to pray to God, face to Face, divested of all created images.

God creates the world, and this creation is a descent. But man's movement towards God is an ascent. In rising from the created world towards God the ascetic does not deny the reality and value of the creation. All he does is not to regard it as an absolute, not to deify it or consider it an end and a value in itself. God did not create the world in order to live the life of the creature: He created it in order to associate man with His own Divine Life. And when man does not arrive at deification, which cannot be achieved without his own collaboration, the very meaning of his existence disappears. Correspondingly, when man, conscious of his divine vocation, contemplates the work of the Creator, he is seized with a wonder which, while giving him a very vivid perception of everything in the created world, at the same time draws him away from every created thing for the sake of contemplating God. This detachment is not a renunciation of created life in the sense of a rejection or denial of it as an illusion. Nor is it a poetic or philosophic flight into a realm of lofty and beautiful images or 'pure' ideas. It is the yearning of love that tugs at the heart-strings and draws man to the living God—the yearning, by virtue of our calling, to live in God, the End of ends and the Value of values. In God is the finality that needs no incarnation, the perfection that excludes all conflict and tragedy. God is not 'beyond good and evil', for He is Light in which there is no shade of darkness.

The simple and humble believer frees himself from the domination of the imagination by a wholehearted aspiration to live according to God's will. This is so simple, and at the same time so 'hidden from the wise and prudent', that it is impossible to explain in words.

The world of human will and imagination is the world of mirages. It is common to man and the fallen angels, and imagination is, therefore, often a conductor of demoniac energy.

Both demoniac images and those conjured up by man may acquire very considerable strength, not because they are real in the ultimate sense of the word, like the Divine Strength which creates out of nothing, but in so far as the human will bows before them. It is only when man gives way that his will is shaped by these images. But repentance liberates from the sway of passion and imagination, and the Christian thus liberated by the Saviour laughs at the power of images.

The power of cosmic evil over man is colossal, and such as no son of Adam can overcome without Christ or outside Christ. He is the Saviour, in the literal and unique sense of the word. This is the Orthodox ascetic's belief, and he therefore pursues the prayer of inner quiet by the unceasing invocation of the Name of Jesus Christ, which is why this prayer is called the Jesus Prayer.

The many manifestations of the imagination which disfigure the spiritual life the Staretz reduced to the four forms indicated above. Of these, the last, where the imagination is given over to creative activity in the theological and philosophical domain, is often so subtle in character that it can even seem to be life in God.

The theologian who is an intellectualist constructs his system as an architect builds a palace. Empirical and metaphysical concepts are the materials he uses, and he is more concerned with the magnificence and logical symmetry of his ideal edifice than that it should conform to the actual order of things.

Strange as it may seem, many great men have been unable to withstand this, in effect, artless temptation, the hidden cause of which is pride. One becomes attached to the fruits of one's intelligence as a mother to her child. The intellectual loves his creation as himself, identifies with it, shuts himself up with it. When this happens no human intervention can help him: if he will not renounce what he believes to be riches he will never attain to pure prayer and true contemplation. Those who seek the highest form of prayer—the uniting of the mind with the heart—know how hard such renunciation is.

Many theologians of the philosophical type, remaining essentially rationalists, rise to suprarational or, rather, supralogical spheres of thought, but these spheres are not yet the Divine world: they lie within the confines of human-created nature and as such are within reach of the understanding in the natural order of things. These mental visions cannot, it is true, be circumscribed within the framework of formal logic, since they go beyond into the domain of metalogic and antinomic reasoning, yet for all that they are still the result of the activity of the reason.

The overcoming of discursive thinking is proof of high intellectual culture but it is not yet 'true faith' and real divine vision. People in this category, who often possess outstanding capacities for rational reflection, come to realise that the laws of human thought are of limited validity, and that it is impossible to encircle the whole universe within the steel hoops of logical syllogisms. This enables them to arrive at a supramental contemplation, but what they then contemplate is still merely beauty created in God's image. Since those who enter for the first time into this sphere of the 'silence of the mind' experience a certain mystic awe, they mistake their contemplation for mystical communion with the Divine. The mind, it is true, here passes beyond the frontiers of time and space, and it is this that gives it a sense of grasping eternal wisdom. This is as far as human reason can go along the path of natural development. At these bounds where 'day and night come to an end' man contemplates a light, which is, however, not the True Light in which there is no darkness, but the natural light peculiar to the mind of man created in God's image.

This mental light, which excels every other light of empirical knowledge, might still just as well be called darkness, for it is the darkness of divestiture and God is not in it. We have been warned by the Lord: 'Take heed therefore that the light which is in thee be not darkness.' The first prehistoric, cosmic catastrophe—the fall of Lucifer, son of the morning, who became the prince of darkness—was due to his enamoured contemplation of his own beauty, which ended in his self-deification.

Those who have stood in these places of the spirit may ask in dismay: 'Where are we to look for a criterion by which to distinguish genuine communion with God from delusion?'

Blessed Staretz Silouan explicitly asserted that we have such a criterion—love for enemies. He said:

'The Lord is meek and humble, and loves His creature. Where the Spirit of the Lord is, there is love for enemies and prayer for the whole world.'

Let no one be so bold as to belittle this canon, for the state it relates to is the direct result of divine action. God saves man utterly. He sanctifies not only his mind but also his psyche with its emotions, and even his body.

We but touch here on the most constant and complex questions pertaining to man's spiritual life—questions which are scarcely capable of a dialectical explanation such as would make them logically intelligible. Only existential experience can bring understanding; but such experience does not depend solely on man's will: it is a gift from on High.

The Christian life is a harmony between two wills, the Divine and the human. God can appear to all men, whatever their course, at every moment in time and in all places. But, Himself beyond constraint, He never forces the freedom of man, His image, and if the creature uses his freedom to turn towards himself in self-love, or to regard himself as the uncreated divine principle, the door will be closed to the action of divine grace, whatever heights of contemplation may be reached.

Communion with God is arrived at through prayer, and this study is precisely a study of prayer. If I enter to a certain extent into the field of dialectics it is not in the hope of convincing by argument but simply to observe that the paths of prayer traverse even this sphere of human thought. Every attempt to rationalise spiritual experience may be met with a variety of objections, because each one of us in the ideal realm of his own contemplation of the world is at liberty to establish whatever scale of values he pleases.

To continue, then, with our inquiry into the subject of prayer, let us examine in broad outline the bitter conflict—the fight against intellectual imagination—which the Orthodox ascetic must engage in if he would progress from prayer which is intellectual meditation to the true prayer of the mind stationed in the heart.

The Orthodox ascetic does not put his trust in his own feeble judgment but in Almighty God. He believes that Christ's commandments are the infallible touchstone, a canon of truth, since they are eternal life itself. This belief stands him on perpetual trial before the Judgment Seat of God, the only true bar of justice. Every deed, every word, every thought or feeling is submitted to the crucible of Christ's word.

When the grace of the Holy Spirit becomes an active force in us our souls naturally incline towards the perfection of the commandments; but when periods of abandonment by God set in, and the Divine Light is replaced by the heavy darkness of the passions in revolt, a great change takes place in us and conflict rends the soul.

The spiritual struggle is a manifold struggle but the struggle with pride strikes deepest and is the most grievous. Pride is the supreme antagonist of divine law, deforming the divine order of being and bringing ruin and death in its train. Pride manifests itself partly on the physical plane but more essentially on the plane of thought and spirit. It arrogates priority for itself, battling for complete mastery, and its principal weapon is the reasoning mind.

In order to assert its superiority the reasoning mind points to its achievements, to its creativeness, producing many convincing proofs purporting to show that in the age-old experience of history the establishment or affirmation of truth falls entirely within its province. Intellectual power is, in fact, one of the energies, one of the manifestations of the human personality. But when this power, functioning according to the impersonal laws of logic, assumes priority in man's spiritual life, it inevitably begins to fight against its source—the hypostatic principle. Then, having overcome this principle within the limits of earthly experience, reason sees itself as trans-personal and universal, and transfers its Idea to the plane of cosmic being, there to seek a sort of supra-personal First Principle.

In its arrogance reason imagines itself ascending to the uppermost heights, descending, as it believes, to the lowest depths. Reason aspires to embrace the integrality of being, in order everywhere to impart its own definition. Failing to attain the confines of being, reason attributes to itself this infinity and ends by identifying itself with the divine principle.

There are some who welcome these claims on the part of reason, who accept them as valid, but the Orthodox ascetic does battle with them. The contest may become tragic and involve extreme tension.

Only through faith can the ascetic win the fight, faith which overcomes the world. 'Whatsoever is born of God overcometh the world: and this is victory that overcometh the world, even our faith.'

There is no comfortable armchair in the study for the monk in his struggle with the reason: in the silence of the night, far from the world, unheard and unseen of others, he falls down before God and weeps the prayer of the publican: 'God be merciful to me a sinner,' or cries with St Peter: 'Lord, save me.'

In spirit the ascetic striver beholds the abyss of 'outer darkness' opening wide before him, and so his prayer is ardent. The struggle may last for years, until the heart is purified of all passion—of pride, first and foremost. Then the Divine Light appears which reveals the falsity of our former judgments—the Light which leads the soul to the limitless expanses of true life.

I had many conversations with the Staretz on this subject. He declared that the trouble lay, not in the reason as such, but in our pride of spirit. Pride strengthens the action of the imagination, whereas humility suspends it. Pride bristles with desire to create its own world, whereas humility is quick to receive life from God.

Long years of warfare had given the Staretz the power to fix his mind steadfastly in God, rejecting all intrusive thoughts. He suffered much in his conflict with the enemy but when I knew him he would speak of the past in great peace of spirit and very simply.

'Mind wrestles with mind . . . our minds with the mind of the enemy . . . The enemy fell through pride and imagination, and would draw us after him . . . We have need of great fortitude in this struggle . . . The Lord 'abandons His servant to the fight and watches him as He watched while St Antony wrestled with evil spirits . . . You remember how in the *Life* of St Antony it says that he took up his abode in a tomb where demons beat him insensible. The friend who looked after the saint then carried him into the village church; but at night, when St Antony recovered consciousness, he entreated his friend to take him back to the tomb. He was too ill to stand, and so prayed lying down. A fresh onslaught of devils beset him. In the midst of cruel tortures, raising his eyes he beheld a great light, and recognised the presence of the Lord; whereupon he said: "Where wert Thou, merciful Jesus, when the enemy were tormenting me?"

'And the Lord answered him:

' "I was here, O Antony, and witnessed thy valour."

'We must always remember that the Lord sees us wrestling with the enemy, and so we need never be afraid. Even should all hell fall upon us we must be brave.

'The Saints learned how to do battle with the enemy. They knew that he uses intrusive thoughts to deceive us, and so all through their lives they declined such thoughts. At first sight there seems to be nothing wrong about an intrusive thought, but soon it diverts the mind from prayer and then stirs up confusion. The rejection of all intrusive thoughts, however apparently good, is therefore essential, and equally essential is it to have a mind pure in God ... But should an intrusive thought approach, there is no cause to be troubled ... Put your trust in God and dwell in prayer ... We must not be troubled, because that rejoices the enemy ... Pray, and the intrusive thought will leave you ... *This is the way of the Saints.'*

The Staretz used to say that there was no end to the pretensions of pride. In his notes I found the following fable:

'A certain huntsman was fond of stalking the woods and fields for game. One day after he had been climbing up a steep hill for hours tracking his prey, exhausted, he sat down on a big stone to rest. Seeing a flight of birds soaring from one summit to another, he began to think: "Why didn't God give me wings that I might fly?" Just then a humble hermit passed by, divined the huntsman's thought and said to him:

' "There you are, sitting and saying to yourself that God has not given you wings; but if you had wings you would still be discontented and say: 'My wings are feeble and I can't fly up to heaven with them, to see what it's like there.' And were you then to be given wings strong enough to lift you to heaven you would still be dissatisfied and say: 'I don't understand what goes on in heaven.' And were you to be given understanding of this you would again be discontented and say: 'Why am I not an angel?' Were you to be turned into a cherubim you would say: 'Why doesn't God let me rule over heaven?' and if it were given you to rule over heaven you would still be dissatisfied and, like another we all know, insolently seek something more. Therefore I tell you, humble yourself at all times, and be content with the gifts you are given. Then you will be living with God."

'The huntsman saw that the hermit spoke the truth, and thanked God for sending him a monk to give him understanding and set him on the path of humility.'

The Staretz insisted that the Saints were concerned, through the humbling of self, to purge the mind of all imagination.

'The Saints all said: "I shall suffer torments in hell"—even though they performed great miracles. They had learned by experience that if the soul condemns herself to hell, but trusts the while in God's compassion, the strength of God enters into her, and the Holy Spirit bears clear witness of salvation. The soul grows humble through self-condemnation, and there is then no place in her for intrusive thoughts, and she stands before God with a pure mind. *This is the wisdom of the spirit.*

With iron drills men drill the earth's crust for oil, and are successful. With their intellectual powers they drill heaven for the fire of divinity, but are rejected of God for their pride.

Divine contemplation is given to man not in those precise moments when he seeks it, and it alone, but when his soul descends into the hell of repentance and does really feel that she is the meanest of creatures. Contemplation forcibly attained through the reason is not true but only seeming contemplation. To accept such contemplation as truth creates conditions in the soul which may prevent the action of grace and make genuine contemplation impossible.

Knowledge revealed in the contemplation which proceeds from grace surpasses the most sublime creations of the imagination, as St Paul affirmed when he said: 'Eye hath not seen, nor ear heard, neither have entered into the heart of man, the things which God hath prepared for them that love him.' When man, as happened to the Apostles, has been transported by grace into a vision of Divine Light, he afterwards translates into theology the things he has seen and known. Authentic theology consists not in the conjectures of man's reason or the results of critical research but in a statement of the life into which man has been introduced by the action of the Holy Spirit. Sometimes words come readily, sometimes it is hard to find the right concepts, the right terms, in which to communicate what is above earthly image and concept. But in spite of these difficulties, and the inevitable existence of various modes of conveying such knowledge, the man who knows by experience will recognise true contemplation even if it be communicated in unfamiliar form, and will distinguish it from illusory, rational conjecture, however brilliant.

8

Uncreated Light and Divine Darkness

THE Uncreated Light is Divine Energy. Contemplation of this Light begets, first and foremost, an all-absorbing feeling of the living God—an immaterial feeling of the Immaterial, an intuitive not a rational perception—which transports man with irresistible force into another world, but so warily that he neither realises when it happens nor knows whether he is in or out of the body. At the time he is more effectively, more deeply conscious of himself than he ever is in everyday life, yet he forgets both himself and the world, carried away by the sweetness of the love of God. In spirit he beholds the Invisible, breathes Him, is wholly in Him.

This supramental sensation of the living God is accompanied by a vision of light, of light essentially different from physical light. Man himself then abides in light, becomes assimilated with the light which he contemplates, and is spiritualised by it. He then neither sees nor feels his own materiality, or the materiality of the world.

The vision comes incomprehensibly. Its approach is unexpected: it appears neither from without nor even from within, but unaccountably encompasses the spirit of man, lifting him into the world of Divine Light; and afterwards he cannot say whether he was in ecstasy—whether his soul had left his body—because he did not notice any return to the body. (Thus there is nothing pathological about his experience.)

God operates, man receives; and space and time, birth and death, sex and age, social or hierarchal status—all cease to exist for him. The Lord has come. In His mercy the Unoriginate Lord of life has come to visit the repentant soul.

Contemplation of Divine Light is unfettered by circumstance: dark of night and light of day are equally propitious. Sometimes the Light comes to man in such fashion that he remains conscious both of his body and of the world around him. He can then stay open-eyed, and simultaneously behold two lights, the physical and the Divine. It is this kind of vision that the holy Fathers called 'vision seen by the physical eyes'. This does not mean, however, that the beholding of Light is analogous to the psycho-physiological process of natural vision, for Divine Light is of a different nature. It is the light of the mind, the light of the spirit, the light of love.

Physical light is the image of Divine Light in the natural world. We can only see the objects around us when there is light, and the eye discerns them badly if the light is poor, better if there is more light, and, finally, in the full light of the sun our vision reaches a certain completeness. Likewise, in the spiritual world no real vision is possible without Divine Light. Divine Light is constant in itself but man's receptivity varies. Faith is light, but in small measure; hope is light, but not yet perfect; the perfect light is love.

Uncreated Light, like the sun, lights up the spiritual world and makes visible the way of the spirit which cannot otherwise be seen. Without this Light man can neither apprehend nor contemplate, still less perform the commandments of Christ, for he dwells in darkness. Uncreated Light bears within it eternal life and the force of divine love. Indeed, it is itself both divine love and divine wisdom, indivisibly one in eternity.

Unless the Divine Light has been contemplated with vigour and intimation, real contemplation has not yet been attained. Whoever rashly anticipates this vision of the Divine Light, relying on his own intellect, will lose himself in contemplation of the mysteries of the Spirit and not only miss them but bar his own way to them. Unpurified by repentance, he will see only the phantoms of truth, created by himself in an arrogant upsurge of logical argument. Spiritual contemplation is not the same thing as abstract intellectual contemplation. Its very nature is different.

Divine Light is eternal life, the kingdom of God, the

uncreated energy of Divinity. It is not contained in created human nature and, being of a different nature, cannot be discovered by ascetic techniques. It comes exclusively as a gift of God's mercy.

Divine Light, omnipresent and in all things, waits upon many, but people 'know him not'. The first advent of Light allows man to see not 'the kingdom of God come with power' but the *nuda veritas* of his own life at that moment: a truth woven of spiritual poverty, servitude, corruption and death. He is brought to the darkness of hell, and the revelation begets ardent, unceasing prayer.

When this prayer for the first time progresses into a vision of Divine Light, what man then contemplates and lives is so novel and unprecedented that he can find no interpretation for it. He feels that the confines of his being have been inexpressibly widened, that the Light has translated him from death to life; but the magnitude of the experience leaves him wondering and bewildered. It is only after repeated visitations that he appreciates the divine gift he has received. At the time of the vision and after, the soul is filled with deep peace and the sweetness of the love of God. She aspires to nothing, neither to glory nor wealth, nor any other earthly happiness, nor even to life itself. All these things seem to her of no account: her entire impulse is towards the living boundlessness of Christ in Whom there is neither beginning nor end; neither darkness nor death.

The Staretz preferred that form of contemplation in which the world is wholly forgotten—in which during imageless prayer the spirit of man is introduced into the domain of limitless light, for such vision gives a greater knowledge of the mysteries of the world to come. In this state the soul lives the full reality of her own participation in divine life—experiences in very truth the advent of God of which the human tongue may not speak. When such a vision comes to an end, as it began, for reasons unknown to man and independent of his will, the soul gently returns to an apprehension of the world around her, and her quiet joy in the love of God is tinged with a lingering sadness at the thought that once more she is about to behold the rough light of the sun.

Man is made in the image of God. What is it that constitutes this image in him? Is it his body? His threefold psychological structure? The answer is extremely complex. Some sort of refraction and reflection of God's image cannot be excluded from the above aspects but the most essential is to be found in the *mode of being*. Created in the image and likeness of God, man is endowed with the capacity to apprehend deification—to receive the divine form of being.

The universe is a marvellous creation but the mystery of the creation of eternal gods is even more prodigious. The divine miracle of man introduced into the world of Uncreated Light strikes on an incomparably deeper level, begetting in us silent wonder before the Face of God.

Blessed Staretz Silouan never spoke of 'darkness' in relation to God, in the same way as from beginning to end of the New Testament—and in the writings of the holy Fathers of the first three centuries of Christianity—there is no mention of 'darkness' as an element in Divine Being or the manifestation of God. He spoke only of the 'darkness of divestiture' into which the soul is plunged during mental prayer, when, by means of particular methods, the ascetic strips himself of all presentment and imaginings, all intellectual concepts, arresting mind and imagination and withdrawing himself from thought of this world.

If we would 'place' this darkness we may say that it lies on the bournes of Uncreated Light. But if the prayer of the soul entering this darkness of divestiture is not powerfully bent on God, free of all presentments (visual and conceptual), she may dwell for a time in this darkness without beholding God, for God is not here inherent in it.

Having arrived at the darkness of divestiture, the mind may feel a peculiar quiet delight, and if it then turns to itself, as it were, it may perceive a certain light, which, however, is not yet the Uncreated Light of Divinity but a natural property of the mind created after God's image. In that it is a crossing of the boundaries of 'things seen which are temporal', such contemplation approaches the mind to knowledge of things which do not 'pass away'—to 'things which are not seen which are eternal'—thereby possessing man of new knowledge, which, nevertheless, is still not eternal life through communion in Divine Being.

The darkness of divestiture is not the sole domain where Divine Light is manifest—God may appear anywhere and to any man, even to those who persecute Him. True, by His appearance He transports man out of this world, and here, too, the consequence is a shedding or divesting of all 'sensible' images and 'intelligible' concepts, but the progression differs.

The man to whom God has deigned to manifest His Uncreated Light will not confuse that Light with the light of his own intellect. The action of Divine Light consumes the passions, and so at certain times (at first, especially) it may be felt as a 'consuming fire'. Every Christian ascetic suffers the burning of this fire.

Divine Being, absolutely realised, absolutely actualised, excludes the presence in Itself of undeveloped potentialities, and, as such, may be defined as *Pure Act*.

Divine Being, as Self-Being, having no cause outside Itself, all-perfect from the beginning, is for the created being *datum* and, as such, may be defined as *Pure Fact*.

As Act (Energy), Divine Being is communicable to the reasoning creature in all Its fulness and infinity. As Fact (Essence), It is absolutely transcendental and incommunicable to the creature, and remains a Mystery, for ever unapproachable.

That the Act of Divine Being is communicable to human nature in all Its fulness was shown by 'the man Christ Jesus', Who is the measure of all things, divine and human, and the ultimate basis for all judgment. St Philip said to Christ: 'Shew us the Father,' and received the answer: 'He that hath seen me hath seen the Father.' But it could also be said: 'He that has seen Christ has seen himself as he should be according to the intention of the Father "before the foundation of the world".'

And just as Christ in His human nature contained 'all the fulness of the Godhead bodily' and 'sat with the Father in his throne', so every man is called to the 'measure of the stature of the fulness of Christ'. If this were not so, Christ could not have bid us 'Be ye therefore perfect, even as your Father which is in heaven is perfect'.

The Saints, fully deified by the gift of grace, are so introduced into the Divine Act that all the attributes of Divinity are imparted to them, even to identity—but identity of Act only, never of Nature. By His Nature God eternally and immutably remains God for created beings, even when they arrive at perfect identity.

Man made in the 'image' of God is created to live, too, 'after His likeness'. God is Omnipresent and Omniscient, and the Saints in Him become omnipresent and omniscient. God is Truth and Life, and the Saints in Him become true and have life. God is absolute Goodness and Love encompassing 'every living substance', and the Saints, in the Holy Spirit, embrace the whole cosmos with their love. The Act of Divine Being is without beginning, and those who are deified, through participation in this Act become without beginning. God is Light in which there is no darkness at all, and the Saints which are His abode He makes pure light. Divine Being is Pure Act, and, when deified, man, in the beginning created as pure potentiality, is completely actualised and he, too, becomes pure act.

The created being of man is wholly dependent upon the Self-Being of the Creator, but participants in the Divine Act become such not in consequence of their 'dependence' but by virtue of free self-determination in the act of perfect love.

The Act of Divine Being is Pure Light. And when the Lord deigns to appear to man He always appears in light and as Light. Holy Scripture declares: 'In thy light shall we see light'; because the vision of Uncreated Divine Light is impossible unless one is in a state of illumination by grace—a state in virtue of which the act of contemplation itself is, above all, 'fellowship with God', union with Divine Life. But when the mind in contemplation of God strives to know God in His Substance, too, it meets with the absolutely impenetrable Mystery of Pure Fact. Contemplation of the incognoscibility of the Divine Nature in the mystical theology of the Fathers is symbolically termed 'Divine darkness'. This term is first encountered in Christian literature in the fourth century, when St Gregory of Nazianzus and St Gregory of Nyssa were obliged to refute the pretensions of certain heretics to know the Substance, too, of God. One of these, Aetios, claimed to know God better than he knew himself, and even sought mathematical definitions for God. The other, Eunomios, avowed that an adequate knowledge of God was possible, and affirmed that he knew God as well as God knew Himself.

The Fathers of the Church called divine darkness 'hyperluminous'. But it must be pointed out that this transcendency relates not to the Uncreated Light, when contemplated, but to the light of every other form of natural knowledge. St Paul expressed man's inability to contain the plenitude of Divine Being when he wrote of 'the Lord of lords ... dwelling in the light which no man can approach unto; whom no man hath seen, nor can see'. And St John the Divine said: 'No man hath seen God at any time; the only begotten Son, which is in the bosom of the Father, he hath declared him'. But the Only-Begotten Son, too, despite His hypostatic incarnation, assumed human nature without any merging of essence, and bides eternally in two natures—unblended, immutable. He 'declared' God in the Act of His Being as Light in which there is no darkness, but did not make known the Substance of God.

9

'Keep thy mind in hell, and despair not'

THE ascetic in spiritual contemplation beholds things which for the overwhelming majority of people are a mystery, but afterwards he is faced with the impossibility of communicating this mystery—translated into mortal language it is construed quite differently by him who hears it. The language of human words and concepts is able only to a very limited extent to convey one man's inner state to another. The indispensable condition for mutual understanding is a common or identical experience. Without it there cannot be understanding because behind our every word lies our whole life. Into every concept each one of us introduces the compass of his own experience, and it is therefore unavoidable that we should speak in different tongues. Yet, since we all share a common nature, it is equally possible to provoke by words a fresh experience in the soul of another, and thus awaken new life in him. If this applies to human intercourse, how much more so does it apply where divine action is involved. The word of God does, in fact, given a certain inner disposition of the soul, offer new life—the eternal life which is contained within it.

No reader of the Gospels can fail to notice the apparent lack of logical sequence in Christ's conversation. Consider, for example, the exchanges with Nicodemus, with the woman of Samaria, with the Disciples at the Last Supper. Christ's interest is directed not so much to what a man says as to what there is in his heart of hearts, and to what he is capable of receiving from God.

Bearing in mind, then, not only the inadequacy but the clumsiness and inaptitude of language as a medium, let us now examine that strange manner of dialogue between God and the Staretz at prayer which concluded with the Staretz hearing within himself the words *Keep thy mind in hell, and despair not*. At first reading there appears to be little of profound significance about this prayer-colloquy. But if we understood its inner meaning, and the force of the revelation given to Silouan, we should be stirred to our very depths. That night the mystery of the fall and the way of redemption were manifest to Silouan.

Keep thy mind in hell, and despair not. What does it mean—to 'keep the mind in hell'? Can it be that we are to use our imagination to conjure up circumstances for ourselves similar to those pictured in some primitive woodcut? No. Father Silouan, like certain great Fathers—St Antony, St Sisoë, St Makarios, St Pimen—during his lifetime actually descended into the darkness and torments of hell. They did this not once but over and over again until their hearts were so permeated that they were able to repeat the movement at will. They took refuge in it when passion—especially that most subtle of passions, pride—reared its head. Informed through long experience that pride separates us from Divine Love, the ascetic, at every manifestation of pride, pours out the vials of his wrath against himself, as unworthy to be with God, and condemns himself to hell, for the flames to consume the power of his every passion.

Blessed Staretz Silouan observed that many spiritual warriors despair when they approach this state (an essential condition for the refining of the passions), and progress no further. But the courageous and experienced ascetic, who knows God's love for us, in his wisdom contrives to stand on the brink of despair while the flames of hell do their work. At the same time he does not fall victim to despair. *And despair not*.

The Staretz' tale is a simple one. But those who have not, on the one hand, undergone the torments of hell and, on the other, experienced great grace, will not measure the full force of his words.

After the night of that supernatural conversation in prayer

the Staretz' long life of spiritual struggle was wholly given up to a search for humility. If we would know the manner and secret of that striving we must meditate on his 'beloved song':

'Soon I shall die, and my accursed soul will descend into hell. There I shall suffer alone in the darkness of the prison-house, and weep with bitter tears: My soul is weary for the Lord and seeks Him in tears. How should I not seek Him? He first sought me and showed Himself to the sinner.'

When he said, 'My accursed soul will descend into hell,' it was no mere figure of speech: he was referring to a real experience of hell—an experience which through the years ate its way into his heart. But when the burning torment has destroyed the passionate thought or feeling he would stay the all-consuming fire by the saving action of the love of Christ, which also he knew and bore within him. *And despair not.*

By constant continuing in this ascetic struggle the soul acquires a certain habit and endurance, and thought of hell becomes so natural that it almost never leaves her.

The Staretz declared: 'The Lord Himself taught me the way to humble myself. "Keep thy mind in hell, and despair not," He said. Thus is the enemy vanquished; but when my mind emerges from the fire the suggestions of passion gather strength again.'

This ascetic 'activity' the great desert Fathers inherited from St Antony. Each of them interpreted the tradition in his own manner but the essence remained the same, a priceless treasure to be handed down the centuries.

At first the experience brings little but personal suffering caused by dwelling in 'outer darkness'. At this stage the ascetic, too, finds himself more or less in the power of hell. But when he sees in himself the light of deliverance from sin there awakens in his soul a mighty compassion for all who 'come short of the glory of God', and prayer for the 'whole Adam' fills his being.

Man's consciousness that he is unworthy of God, and his condemnation of himself for every sin, in strange fashion makes him kin with the Spirit of Truth, and sets his heart free for divine love. And with the increase of love and the light of truth comes revelation of the mystery of the redeeming descent into hell of the Son of God. Man himself becomes more fully like Christ; and through this likeness to Christ in the 'impoverishment' (κένωσις) of His earthly being he becomes like to Him also in the fulness of Eternal Life. God embraces all things, even the bottomless abysses of hell, for there is no domain outside His reach, and the Saints behold and abide in hell, but it has no power over them, and the manner of their abiding differs from the abiding of those who constitute hell.

The Lord's bidding to the Staretz—*Keep thy mind in hell, and despair not*—reveals the unique path to complete purification and divine love. This is the unmysterious mystery of the Saints.

10

The Death of the Staretz

ONE cannot live a Christian life: all one can do is to 'die daily' in Christ, like St Paul.

My attempt to describe something of the great Staretz' spiritual path brings me now to his end. The last years of his life were spent in perpetual prayer for the world. Outwardly he continued tranquil and unvarying but his eyes now often held a thoughtful, sad expression. Again and again he would revert to two themes: ' "I go unto my Father, and your Father; and to my God, and your God." ... Just think what a compassionate saying that is ... The Lord makes us all one family.' And the other: 'Pray for people ... pity the people of God.'

When I remarked that it was hard to pray for people he replied: 'Of course it is hard ... To pray for people is to shed blood. But we must pray none the less. Everything that grace has ever taught must be performed to the end of one's life ... The Lord at times forsakes the soul in order to prove her, that she may testify her understanding and free will; but if a man does not constrain himself to pray he will lose grace, whereas if he evinces good will grace will love him and abandon him no more.'

It was clear that 'grace had come to love' Staretz Silouan and leave him no more. But whither does grace lead?

In the structure of the world we perceive a hierarchical order, a division into upper and lower—a pyramid of being. Yet the idea of equality is deeply rooted in our consciousness and will not be denied.

Some, observing the psycho-physical world, for the one part, and the actual spiritual state of humanity, for the other, and remarking in both a pyramid of inequality, accept the hierarchical pattern as inevitable. Others, inspired by the spirit's profound urge and feeling for equality, strive to realise it in the moral existence of mankind. But centuries of human history would seem to prove that there can be no equality where the fundamental principle of existence is personal freedom.

What, then, can be done to alter this state of affairs, so inacceptable to the Christian conscience? We cannot ignore our longing to see all men equal in the fulness of divine life, in the likeness of the Holy Trinity in Whom there is neither first nor last, neither greater nor lesser. Let us see how Christ resolved the dilemma.

Christ does not deny the fact of inequality, of division into upper and lower, into overlord and servant; but He turns the pyramid upside down and thus achieves perfection. He, the apex of the pyramid, said of Himself that He 'came not to be ministered unto, but to minister, and to give his life a ransom for many'. He bade His disciples follow the example He offered when He washed their feet. 'Ye know,' He told them, 'that the princes of the Gentiles exercise dominion over them, and they that are great exercise authority upon them. But it shall not be so among you: but whosoever will be great among you, let him be your minister; and whosoever will be chief among you, let him be your servant.'

Here we are shown both the designation and the meaning of the ecclesiastical hierarchy—to raise those low in the spiritual scale to a higher degree of perfection. 'And he gave some, apostles; and some, prophets; and some, evangelists; and some, pastors and teachers; For the perfecting of the saints, for the work of the ministry, for the edifying of the body of Christ: Till we all come in the unity of the faith, and of the knowledge of the Son of God, unto a perfect man, unto the measure of the stature of the fulness of Christ.'

When abundant grace touches the heart, the Christian, animated by the love of Christ acting in him, really does descend to the base of the upturned pyramid, where the crushing weight is concentrated—to the place where the Lord is, Who took upon Himself the sins of the world.

The most effective form of service to the world is prayer.

The ascetic's personal tribulation inspires his heart with compassionate love for all who suffer. His mind, his heart, even his body—his entire being—are drawn to God in fervent prayer for people, sometimes individuals, known or unknown, sometimes for all mankind down the ages. This kind of prayer undoubtedly influences the whole course of the history of the world, modifying not only historical but cosmic events, too. Such prayer is repentance for the sins of men and, *quâ* repentance, means to a certain extent bearing the burdens of the world. But man in the flesh, at this stage of his life, is always bound by the conditions of earthly existence, and so all his actions carry a relative imprint. Perfection can be attained only through the great mystery of death, which either sets the seal of eternal truth on the path taken through life or, on the contrary, unmasks its falsehood. Death, as the destruction of the organic life of the body, is the same for everyone, but as a spiritual event it has a peculiar purport and significance for each one of us.

On Thursday, 2/15 September 1938, towards five o'clock in the morning (around 11 a.m. by Athonite time) I went to see the Staretz in the storehouse, and found him serene as always. He spoke in his normal, level tones, and I noticed nothing unusual. He was busy with his everyday work.

At about ten in the morning, after lunch, I went to see him in his cell. He was seated on a stool by his table, and I saw that all was not well.

'Staretz, what is the matter?'

'I feel ill.'

'What is wrong?'

'I do not know.'

He got up and sat heavily on his bed, leaning back against the wall and propping himself up in a half-reclining position with his right arm. Then he gradually straightened his neck, lifted his head and an expression of pain settled on his face.

I said: 'Staretz, are you going to die?'

'I have not yet learned humility.'

He slowly drew his feet up on to the bed, let his head slide down on to the pillow and lay there as he was, fully dressed. After a short silence I spoke again:

'Staretz, you ought to go to the infirmary.'

'I would rather not. There are people there, and besides they would put me by the clock again, like last time, and its ticking disturbs my prayer.'

'But you cannot stay here ill. Who is there to look after you? You would be more comfortable in hospital.'

'If they would give me a room to myself, I would go.'

I left him, saying I would speak to Father Thomas, who ran the infirmary.

The two-storeyed monastery hospital was divided into an upper and a lower ward. The lower ward consisted of one large room partitioned into two with, at one end, by the windows which looked out over the sea, a couple of tiny rooms screened off by thin partitions. Father Thomas put one of these at the disposal of the Staretz.

When I went back and told him this, he consented to go but by then was so ill that he could no longer walk by himself, and had to be supported. Sadly I helped him along to the infirmary.

The monastery hospital has no technical apparatus for making diagnoses, and nobody determined what was wrong with the Staretz. His condition grew rapidly worse. Following the custom in cases of serious illness, he took communion every day; and on Monday, September 6/19 he received the last anointing.

I went often to see him but could not bring myself to disturb him by talking. I simply sat outside in the ward by his half-open door, for his room was very small. I had had frequent occasion to see how the Staretz lived, and had heard from his lips much that gave me a picture of his inner spiritual life. I was able to a certain extent to watch how he approached the great mystery of death, but the actual moment of his passing was hidden from me.

During the last days of his life, from the beginning of his illness to his end, the Staretz was silent. Before, he used to tell me how a certain *schema-monk* lay in the infirmary preparing for death, never opening his eyes lest any outward impression trouble his thought of God; and when a close friend and fellow-ascetic whom he loved came to see him he said a few brief words to him with his eyes shut, having recognised him by his voice. I remembered this and, with rare exceptions, did not violate the Staretz' tranquillity with questions.

A week elapsed and the Staretz' state became critical. On the Friday evening, September 10/23, shortly before sunset, Father-confessor Sergii came to see him, to read over him the *Canon of the Mother of God* for the departure of the soul, called the *Canon for the Dying*. The confessor went up to the sick man's bed and said:

'Give the blessing, Father Silouan.'

The Staretz opened his eyes and gazed at us in tender silence. His face looked pale and ill but peaceful. When the priest saw that he was silent he asked him:

'Well, Father Silouan, do you know us?'

'I do,' answered the Staretz in a low but distinct voice.

'And how do you feel?'

'Well. Very well.'

Was this answer an expression of an ascetic desire to hide his sufferings by not complaining of his sickness, or did the Staretz actually feel so well spiritually that he no longer realised his illness, which did not infringe on his peace of soul? I do not know.

'We have come to pray with you and read you the *Canon of the Mother of God* ... Would you like that?' asked the spiritual father.

'Yes ... Thank you ... I would like that very much.'

Father Sergii began to read the Canon. The Staretz lay pale and quiet, on his back, his eyes closed, mctionless. His right arm lay across his breast; his left by his side. Without moving his left hand, I cautiously found and felt his pulse. It was very weak, and so irregular that it changed several times in half a minute.

The reading of the Canon drew to a close. The Staretz opened his eyes again and softly thanked us. We left him, bidding him farewell 'till morning'.

At midnight Father Nikolai, the infirmarian, went into the Staretz' room. The Staretz asked him:

'Is that matins they are reading?'

'Yes,' answered Father Nikolai, and added: 'Do you need anything?'

'No, thank you, nothing.'

The quiet manner in which the Staretz asked his question of Father Nikolai, and then answered him, and the fact that he could hear matins which were barely audible in his corner, shows that he was conscious and in full possession of himself. When matins were over—that is, about an hour and a half later—and the infirmarian looked in again, the Staretz had passed away. Nobody had heard a sound, not even those who lay near him, so gently did he go to God.

STARETZ SILOUAN, PRAY TO GOD FOR US